THE GALLAGHER GUIDE

TO THE BABY YEARS

THE GALLAGHER GUIDE TO THE BABY YEARS

THE REAL MOMS' SURVEY OF TOP-RATED PRODUCTS AND ADVICE

2005 EDITION

Edited by Stephanie Gallagher

ATRIA BOOKS / New York   London   Toronto   Sydney

ATRIA BOOKS
1230 Avenue of the Americas
New York, NY 10020

ISBN: 0-7434-8476-2

First Atria Books trade paperback edition October 2004

Book design by Liney Li

10   9   8   7   6   5   4   3   2   1

ATRIA BOOKS is a trademark of Simon & Schuster, Inc.

Manufactured in the United States of America

For information regarding special discounts for bulk purchases,
please contact Simon & Schuster Special Sales at 1-800-456-6798 or
business@simonandschuster.com

Acknowledgments

THERE ARE MANY PEOPLE without whom this book would not have been possible. I am extremely grateful to the amazing mommies who contributed their wisdom, insight, and experience to make *The Gallagher Guide to the Baby Years* a reality. Chrys Li deserves a huge thanks for her arduous work in putting together the database and doing an awesome job in managing the surveys. Like a true expert, you always made it seem so easy. Al Ries brought his own special brand of marketing savvy to bear on this book—the kind of savvy that has made him an icon. Without you, I wouldn't have this title. George Silverman played an important role in the development of this book. Without you and your fantastic work, there would never be a Gallagher Guide. Many, many thanks! To my agent, Eileen Cope, thanks for your early enthusiasm and unwavering commitment. You're a true pro. My sincerest thanks to Frank Fochetta and your team in special sales. You're tops with me. And finally, to Tracy Behar, who instinctively got the vision, and worked harder than I could imagine in making that vision a reality. You're a rare breed of editor, Tracy. There aren't many around like you. I feel so lucky to have you.

For my two "creeps."

You know who you are.

Now go to bed.

CONTENTS

INTRODUCTION

Being a mom is an awesome responsibility. You literally have the opportunity to create the future. The possibilities are inspiring.

The important thing to remember is that not only does your child's future rest in your hands, it depends on the decisions you make today. So if your baby grows up to be an ax murderer, it's probably because you chose to bottlefeed. Or let him sleep in your bed. Or screwed up pottytraining.

KIDDING!

Listen, a lot of people take this mommy thing way too seriously. Okay, you've probably figured out that this mom thing isn't all cottony soft skin nuzzling and watching your baby coo. It's serious stuff. Like learning that your car seat has to be installed by a professional who has taken a two-week course to learn how to do it right, and discovering what a lactation consultant is and that knowing one may mean the difference between agony and bliss for you in those first few weeks of motherhood.

What you may not know is that it doesn't have to be overwhelming. Here's a secret: You can learn everything you need to know to be a fantastic mother with a single shortcut. Even better: It is available to you right here, right now, and taking it won't make a bit of difference in your baby's future. Well, other than the fact that she probably won't get into Harvard because you opted for the *Cliffs Notes*™ course in motherhood.

Again, KIDDING!

So what's the secret? Other mommies! Other mommies can tell you everything you need to know to become the absolutely fabulous mom you were born to be. From how to put together that 347-piece activity gym that came with no instructions to where to go to get the best baby pictures taken.

Which brings us to this book. In *The Gallagher Guide to the Baby Years,* you'll learn all that and more. Quite simply, *The Gallagher Guide to the Baby Years* is a mommy group in a box (well, between two covers anyway), replete with indispensable ratings from the absolute best convertible car seat to our top proven methods for coping with nursing soreness.

To put together *The Gallagher Guide,* we surveyed nearly two hundred moms (including doctor moms) from all over the world, and brought you all of their best advice in one place. Before *The Gallagher Guide,* the only way to acquire this precious tribal wisdom was through trial and error—or in the ladies room at Nordstrom. (If you haven't had the privilege of experiencing Nordstrom's bathroom firsthand, you must make a pilgrimage there immediately. It is quite possibly the single most comfortable environment to change and feed a baby known to womankind.)

But you can't just sit around a department store bathroom hoping to glean child-rearing advice, right? Well, maybe you can. But it isn't the most efficient way to gather mommy intelligence, and it does limit your findings to a small circle of women. In *The Gallagher Guide to the Baby Years,* you get all this wonderful wisdom in one easy reference that you can turn to again and again.

We've park-tested strollers for durability and sound-tested children's music for listenability. We've learned all the secrets, tricks, and little-known tips that only veteran moms know for everything from coaxing a burp out of a gassy baby to getting name-brand baby clothes at rock-bottom prices.

The truth is our homes, cars, playgrounds, and parks are the most rigorous testing labs in the world, and that's where our advice has been invented, tested, and proven to work.

The Gallagher Guide to the Baby Years is the first book to take the product reviews, time-saving secrets, and mom-savvy shortcuts that have been learned in the trenches and put them on paper, all in one place, rated and categorized for easy reference. We hope you enjoy this treasury of top-rated products and tips, and that you'll share with us your comments and suggestions for future editions. E-mail us at survey@soundbitepress.com with your ideas. We look forward to hearing from you.

TO CONTRIBUTE TO THE NEXT EDITION, VISIT WWW.GALLAGHERGUIDE.COM

THE GALLAGHER GUIDE

TO THE BABY YEARS

CHAPTER ONE

Pregnancy

Oh, the aches and pains of it all! We may love the idea of growing a human being, but pregnancy also means morning sickness, weight gain, stretch marks, leg cramps, and an inability to go more than twenty minutes without peeing (okay, not really, but it feels like that).

The worst part about going through it the first time is that you don't know what to expect. Then, when you go through it again, you're a veteran, except you discover that every pregnancy is different (if you didn't have morning sickness the first time, you could have it for nine months the second), and that your body doesn't bounce back nearly as fast as it did the first time. Here is our best wisdom for getting through those nine (really, ten) months with ease.

The Five Most Effective Ways to Cope with Morning Sickness

1. Crackers, especially Saltines and especially when eaten first thing in the morning.
2. Ginger anything—ginger ale, ginger tea, ginger snaps.
3. Lemon anything—lemon drops, lemonade, lemon verbena oil, lemons.
4. Eat small, frequent meals.
5. Eat protein.

"I'm on an e-mail loop of moms, and one of the ladies suggested ginger. Anything with ginger works. I liked ginger snaps because they put a little something in my stomach, and that helps morning sickness also. But you can get ginger candy and gum also. It's the best-kept secret."
—Brenda Brown, Kapolei, HI

"One of the many books I read when I was trying to conceive mentioned that lemons, lemon drops, and lemon oil can be helpful in taming nausea. I purchased lemon verbena oil (an essential oil you can get at any health food store) the weekend I found out I was pregnant. It smells like very concentrated lemons. I would just crack the top on the vial of oil and sniff anytime I felt sick. Ninety-nine percent of the time, my stomach would calm right down. It worked wonders."
—Colleen Grace Weaver, San Lorenzo, CA

"I had horrible morning sickness until about week 18. I craved protein and bought a Burger King egg and cheese bagel or croissant almost every morning. The sandwiches tasted great and I didn't have to smell the eggs cooking."
—Kimberly Mercurio, M.D., Downers Grove, IL

"I always tried to make sure I had something in my stomach. It helped to munch on crackers, bread, etc., and to drink lots of water."
—Stephanie Zara, Boonton Township, NJ

"Eat something (like a cracker or two) BEFORE getting out of bed (have someone bring it to you, or leave it on your nightstand the night before). It always seemed easier to avoid nausea by eating little amounts frequently than to stop nausea once it starts."
—Chelsea Hamman, M.D., Providence, NC

TO CONTRIBUTE TO THE NEXT EDITION,
VISIT WWW.GALLAGHERGUIDE.COM

Nine Easy Ways to Relieve Heartburn and Acid Reflux

Just when you thought you were past the hard part—the morning sickness—bam! You get hit with heartburn. Some of us had it through our whole pregnancies. But there's no need to wait for the baby to be born to get relief. Here are our nine favorite remedies.

1. Take Tums or another over-the-counter heartburn remedy (with your doctor's approval).
2. Elevate your head and shoulders while sleeping.
3. Drink lots of water.
4. Avoid spicy foods.
5. Eat smaller, more frequent meals.
6. Eat sour foods, like lemonade or sour candy.
7. Eat popsicles.
8. Try papaya extract or papaya enzyme (with your doctor's permission).
9. Drink milk.

"Take Tums antacid tablets every day. My obstetrician recommended it for the calcium and the heartburn."
—Jennifer Young, Bethesda, MD

"I raised the head of my bed four inches and slept with a pillow wedge to keep upright. I also stayed away from tomato-based foods."
—Becky Messerli, Chesterfield, MI

"I don't believe in taking medications at all. I try to treat everything naturally, so what I would do is not eat until I was full. Also, I would eat smaller meals often. I never ate and lay down, and I drank tons of water."
—Jaimelin Liddell, Roseto, PA

"Anything sour will help with heartburn and nausea. I ate sour ball candy and drank a lot of lemonade."
—*Wendy Douglas, Margate, FL*

"My cousin's mother-in-law is a 'Holistic Healer' and recommended taking papaya extract for heartburn and acid reflux. You can find it in most health food stores. Some may even carry a chewable tablet, kind of like Chicklets. Not only do they kick heartburn and acid reflux, but they are pretty tasty as well. I'd recommend them to anyone, pregnant or not."
—*Lamiel Oesterreicher, Brooklyn, NY*

Your Essential Maternity Wardrobe

The best thing about early pregnancy is that you get to keep it a secret if you like. You get to decide who to tell, when to tell, and how to break the good news. By the fourth or fifth month, however, it's no longer a secret. And if you haven't noticed it yet, you begin to get distracted by the fact that NOTHING IN YOUR CLOSET FITS YOU ANYMORE. What to do? Veteran moms know that being comfortable is key. Regardless of the season, you'll need a basic wardrobe that will take you from work to play to evening in comfort.

THE ONLY FIVE RULES YOU NEED TO KNOW FOR BUYING MATERNITY CLOTHES

1. Make it comfortable.
2. Make it black.
3. Good underwear, including a good bra, is essential.
4. Buy pieces that don't have the maternity panel or a seam in the tummy area.
5. Invest in one nice outfit for special occasions and dinners out.

"Think about whether some of your maternity clothes can be worn after you have the baby. They make no-panel and low-rise pants

now that are great for that transitional period when you're too big for your old clothes and not big enough to keep wearing panel maternity pants."
—*Angel Smith, Brooksville, FL*

"I loved being pregnant and wanted the world to know, so I loved wearing the obvious 'maternity clothes' look. However, the most important items in my pregnant wardrobe were hardly ever seen. The real essentials include a super-comfortable, front latch, all-cotton (if you can find it) sleeping bra! Your ever-growing breasts can be painful, especially at night as you toss and turn. A good sleeping bra (similar to an exercise or jogging bra) can keep your breasts supported and lessen the discomfort.

"Comfortable panties are another must, and I found gigantic briefs to do the trick, as long as they were big enough to go completely over the belly. Anything hitting the waistline was torture. After my pregnancy, I was told by friends that they liked bikinis for the same reason (they didn't restrict the waistline).

"Whether or not you are one of the women whose feet swell in pregnancy, near the end of the pregnancy, you will find bending over to be less than fun. Bending over to tie your shoes will be downright annoying. Take care of your comfort and sanity by having comfortable slip-on shoes or sandals that you can manage to slip in and out of without help!"
—*Theresa Smead, St. Louis, MO*

"Those pants with the stretch panels were a definite no-no for me. The seam where the panel was connected to the non-stretch fabric always cut into my belly. I got one of those wardrobe-in-a-box sets that was great, came with a short skirt, leggings, a jumper dress, and two shirts (short sleeve and long sleeve). Comfy and stylish!"
—*Michele Longenbach, Garden Grove, CA*

"I resisted buying maternity underwear with my first pregnancy, [but later when I tried them] I couldn't believe how much more comfortable (although ugly) they were."
—*Tammy McCluskey, M.D., Kinnelon, NJ*

"There are times when you just don't want anything touching your tummy, and even if it has the elastic maternity panel in front, it still irritates you. Baby doll dresses work best."
—*K. Scarlett Shaw, Euless, TX*

"First, black pants. I worked in an office and I would wear those pants every day. No one ever noticed! They were so comfortable and went with everything. Second, comfy, slip-on shoes. I gave up trying to tie my shoes somewhere around the sixth month. Third, supportive bras. I knew I was pregnant when my chest exploded. Supportive bras are the best investment."
—*Sara Hammontree, Mountain Home, AR*

"I recommend Lands' End leggings. You can buy them in normal sizes. I got the "Tall" sizing—it gives you more length from crotch to waistband. I also got a large. Believe it or not, they stretched to accommodate me in my ninth month and also my usual size before and after. They were supportive immediately postpartum, too."
—*Sarah Pletcher, East Lansing, MI*

The Five Hottest Places to Buy Maternity Clothes

Gone are the days of baby doll dresses and big floppy bows. Today, maternity clothes come in the same fashionable styles as regular women's clothes, and you don't need to go to a fancy boutique or spend a lot of money to get them. Indeed, many of the same stores where you normally shop now carry maternity clothes. Here are our favorites.

1. Target
2. The Gap
3. Old Navy
4. Motherhood Maternity
   (and Motherhood Maternity Outlet)
5. eBay

"Motherhood Maternity is fairly priced, and the quality of their clothes is decent (they do tend to shrink quite quickly, so be careful when drying). Target is also a good choice for maternity wear. They now sell the Liz Lange line, which is nice. I would actually wear some of the clothes even if I wasn't pregnant."
—*Katie Conroy, Palos Hills, IL*

"I bought many of my maternity clothes off of eBay. It's a great way to get all the clothes you need without spending an arm and a leg. Maternity clothes are too expensive to buy a whole new wardrobe that will only last a few months."
—*Jonalee Fernatt, Ulrichsville, OH*

"Target maternity clothes are affordable, look nice, and last."
—*Sara Dixon, Grimesland, NC*

"JCPenney.com and Motherhood Maternity Outlet both have great selections of plus-sized maternity clothes, and they are pretty inexpensive. The Motherhood outlet stores seem to have a much better selection of plus-sized clothes. Also, watch for rummage sales. I bought around thirty items of plus-sized maternity clothes in great condition for $27!"
—*Amy McDonald, Buffalo, MN*

"Old Navy and Gap Maternity can both be found online (some Old Navy stores carry maternity also). They offer free returns and exchanges, so sizes are not that big of a deal to try before you know what will work. With my first pregnancy, I ordered and paid for shipping one time, then just continued exchanging so much that I never had to pay for shipping again! The clothes are similar to 'normal' clothes (not tentlike pregnancy stuff) and fit very well."
—*Kari Rydell, Ladera Ranch, CA*

"Target has really stylish clothes that last the whole pregnancy, plus the prices are perfect! Also, don't be afraid to shop online. I bought over fifty articles of maternity clothing in a lot on eBay

with my last pregnancy, all for $115! There were a couple of things in there that I wouldn't wear, but the rest were perfect!"
—*Stephanie R. Smith, Alexandria, KY*

Our Seven-Step Formula for Coping with Bed Rest

In the first trimester, you fantasize about being put on bed rest. You're *sooooo* tired, you think, hmmm, forced to stay in bed? Sign me up! But being confined to your bed during pregnancy can be lonely, boring, and emotionally draining. Here are the best ways to cope.

1. Accept it.
2. Stock up on books, magazines, and videos.
3. Arrange a schedule for visitors.
4. Get a laptop computer and join an online support group for expectant moms.
5. Ask for help with cooking, cleaning, running errands, finishing the baby's room.
6. Do simple craft projects.
7. Get dressed and put on makeup (if you normally wear it) every day.

"If finances allow, get a laptop computer. You can make family picture albums, keep in touch with relatives, meet new cyber-friends who are in the same boat, study up on fetal development, and so much more. If you have a DVD player, there is an online rental service called Netflix that can be a sanity-saver. For around $20 a month, you get up to three DVDs that you can exchange as much as you like or keep as long as you like. No late fees or trips to the video store, and since it takes about four to five days for you to receive a new one after sending one back, you can have a new movie almost every night if you stagger them. They even provide postage-paid mailers."
—*Angel Smith, Brooksville, FL*

"Ask family and friends for help with meals, finishing the nursery, and running errands. Though your spouse can do those things as well, he will more than likely still be working 40+ hours per week and tending to some of your other needs.

"Each day, set up your beds: your normal one and one on the couch. Have plenty of fluids and prepared snacks, get a good book, have lots of pillows and a blanket, and keep the phone close by. Relax and don't stress about the things that are not getting done. You are doing the most important thing: taking care of the baby."
—*Dana A. Croy, Murfreesboro, TN*

"Have friends and neighbors work out a visitation/cooking rotation, so that you don't have six visitors and nine casseroles in one day, then nothing for a week.

"Don't think you're going to use this time to learn Russian, knit an afghan, or balance your checkbook. Bed rest fries your brain; you will be lucky to concentrate long enough to finish a magazine.

"Change out of your pajamas every morning. Comb your hair and put on a touch of makeup. If you lie around looking like a sick person, you're going to start to feel like a sick person.

"Have a friend come over to paint your toenails or cut/style your hair. It'll make you feel sooooo much better! If your partner isn't cleaning the house to your satisfaction and the dishes and laundry are piling up, let it go! If you absolutely cannot stand the filth for one more second, pick up the phone and recruit some friends, family, or a maid service to tidy up.

"Make sure that your partner or spouse gets some time for himself as well. A game of basketball or beer with his buddies after work will do wonders for his stress level and make him much more willing to pitch in at home.

"Finally, don't cheat on your bed rest! I know lots of mommies who thought, 'Well, one little outing won't hurt,' or 'My doctor will never know,' who wound up in the hospital and/or with babies in the Neonatal Intensive Care Unit. This is the one time in your life when doing absolutely nothing is the best thing you can do for your child."
—*Jenna Haldeman, Portland, OR*

"Arrange visitors if you feel up to it. Having someone bring you lunch on the couch is a great day-brightener. People may ask what they can do for you. Make a list of errands you need to have done and dole them out to well-meaning friends. Call people if you are a chatty person. I found that even five minutes on the phone with a friend gave me a boost.

"If you are only on limited bed rest (you can still be upright some of the time), find an online community. BabyCenter.com and other pregnancy-related websites have groups that are for folks on bed rest.

"Finally, remember how important the work of growing a baby is. Sure, there are people out there who are doing their jobs, earning a living, or enjoying their leisure time, but you made ears or eyebrows or toenails or a heart muscle or a brain cell today. Now how many people can say that?"
—*Amelia Stinson-Wesley, Morganton, NC*

Four Scrumptious, Healthy Pregnancy Snacks

1. Fruit . . . by itself, with cottage cheese, in a shake or smoothie
2. Peanut butter and . . . crackers, wheat bread, celery, carrots, banana, jelly, pretzels, apples, bagels
3. Yogurt
4. Raw vegetables and dip

"I craved spinach salads, topped with grape tomatoes, feta cheese, and blue cheese dressing. Lots of calcium, which may help with preterm labor, good amount of calories, and it's not too heavy to eat through those days of nausea."
—*Traci Bragg, M.D., Jacksonville, FL*

"I had chocolate organic yogurt. It really helped me make it through pregnancy without caffeine and still keep awake at work."
—*Beth Blecherman, Menlo Park, CA*

"I liked frozen green grapes."
—*Chantal Laurin, Concord, Ontario, Canada*

"Prunes. I ate a ton of the lemon- and orange-flavored ones. Not only do they have a lot of iron, but they help alleviate constipation."
—*Sara Hammontree, Mountain Home, AR*

"I kept a ton of stuff at my desk during work. I tried to keep semi-healthy things—wheat thins, pretzels, dried cereal, dried fruit, Chex mix, yogurt. I also kept orange juice, water, and fruit in the fridge. I really think this helped to keep down the weight gain."
—*Brandy Charles, Tulsa, OK*

"I ate a lot of veggie roll-ups with cream cheese, spinach leaves, roasted red peppers, shredded carrots, and scallions on a tortilla. When I wanted more protein, I added slices of chicken."
—*Patricia Arnold, Westford, MA*

"Strawberries, banana, vanilla pudding and milk in the blender is a fantastic breakfast on the run or late-night snack . . . and helps you get the fruits and calcium that seem hard to get enough of."
—*Rebecca Curtis, Oshawa, Ontario, Canada*

"I liked yogurt with granola mixed in and raw veggies. I didn't really eat any more than when I wasn't pregnant, so I had to make sure the food I was getting was good food. I would bring raw veggies with dip into work and keep them on my desk for easy snacking."
—*Genevieve Molloy, Guttenberg, NJ*

"I lived on peanut butter. It gave me the extra protein I needed for my twins. I made a sandwich and wrapped it, and I kept it at my bedside for those hungry times in the middle of the night. It hit the spot!"
—*Lori Vance, Henderson, NV*

The No-Lose Way to Pick the Perfect Baby Name

As your belly grows, so does the reality that there actually is another human being growing in there, and this little one is going to need a name. Choosing a baby name is a sometimes delicate, sometimes frustrating, and always meaningful endeavor, since everyone seems to place a major importance on it. If your in-laws aren't determined to have you name the kid after some long-lost dead relative, your own parents are pushing you to use a family name, your spouse is dying to have the baby named after him, or friends are quick to weigh in with their own preferences and aversions. This is what we've learned in handling the name game.

1. Keep it a secret!
2. Consider how your child will feel about the name years from now—is it difficult to pronounce? Will she be teased because it sounds funny or rhymes with certain words?
3. Don't try to please other people—only you and your partner need to agree.
4. Check the initials to make sure they aren't problematic.
5. Decide in advance or at least have a couple of names under consideration before you go to the hospital.

"When my husband and I decided on a name for our son (we knew it was a boy), we kept the name a secret. It took a long time to decide, and we did not want others' opinions to influence our decision. People don't mind telling you if they hate the name before the baby is born, then telling you what you should name it. After the baby is born, it is too late, and everyone tells you what a great name you picked, no matter what!"
—Kristi Swartz, Gaithersburg, MD

"Everyone wants you to name the baby after them. Remember, you can't please everyone, so don't try. Name your baby with a name you like and a name your baby will hopefully want to live with for the rest of your baby's life. You should also think about the initials. For a not-so-cool example, William Eugene Thompson spells W.E.T. Unfortunately, my brother, trying to please the grandparents, named his son this name and he has been teased terribly."
—*Barbara Nichols, Okeechobee, FL*

"Say the name (first and last) out loud and make sure it sounds good. Write it down and make sure it doesn't look or sound like any word(s) that will be embarrassing to you later. Once you have picked a name you like, don't share it with family members. They may want to offer their own opinions and may actually try to dissuade you from the name you have spent a great deal of time deciding upon. I wished I had just kept quiet about it until after my baby was born. It would've been easy just to say that we were still thinking about our options."
—*Krystal Johnston, M.D., Manistee, MI*

"Our daughters were not named until right before we left the hospital! We had not really discussed it at length and when we did, we could not agree. We love the names we chose, but it's best to select when you're not under pressure."
—*Shannon Guay, Galloway, OH*

"Don't be afraid to go with a name that you love. My daughter's name is Reagan. Many people frowned at it, told me how bad it was, and how much they hated it. People also ask if she is named after President Reagan. I always loved the name and that is why it is hers. Now she is two, and people who hated it tell me they love it and can't imagine her as anything else."
—*Susan Dobratz, Plymouth, MA*

CHAPTER TWO

THE ESSENTIAL NURSERY

S ometime after the morning sickness sub-
sides and before the contractions start, it's
a good idea to start thinking about where
this kid is going to sleep. Baby furniture, like
most furniture, typically has to be ordered, and it can
take several months to get certain styles. Also, if you get
the crib early, you'll be able to get it put together and set
up at your leisure, which will give you one less thing to
think about after the baby arrives.

The Five Most Important Items for Your Baby's Nursery

1. CRIB

A crib should be your first purchase. And when shopping for a crib, safety should be your number one con-
cern. This is one item you definitely want to purchase
new. Safety standards change all the time, so you cannot
be sure that the crib you found at the local consignment
shop or borrowed from Aunt Martha meets current
guidelines. Sure, Aunt Martha will swear that it got her
through three children just fine, but then again, she
also probably installed her own car seats (something we
now know should be done by a professional) or didn't
have them at all!

It's also a good idea to test the drop-down side before you buy, especially if you're on the petite side. If you're over 5' 4" or so, you'll probably be able to easily lift your baby in and out of the crib without even lowering the side at first, but eventually, your baby will sit up and you'll have to lower the crib mattress, making it necessary to lower the side to get your baby.

Since you'll be lowering the side several times a day, you want to make sure it works smoothly. Can it be done with one hand? Finally, what kind of sound does it make when you raise the side? The quieter the better, as there will be many times the baby will be asleep when you lay him down, and you'll want to be able to raise the crib side without waking him up.

If money is tight, consider whether or not you really need the extra features, like a drawer underneath the crib or the ability to convert it to a toddler bed. These extras make the crib more expensive, and you may end up not using them.

Check to see how easy it is to lower the mattress. You will have to do this several times as the baby begins to crawl, stand, and yes, even try to climb out of the crib. So you want a crib with a mattress support that's as easy to lower as possible. Snug and firm should be your watchwords when shopping for a mattress. You don't want any gaps between the mattress and the crib slats.

As for bedding, we recommend you buy a waterproof mattress pad and at least two, preferably three, crib sheets. That way you'll always have extra sheets handy if one is in the wash.

Other crib accessories, such as bumpers, a skirt, and a mobile are optional, but they do look awfully darned cute. Of course, pillows, comforters, and fluffy toys are definite no-nos, as they pose a suffocation hazard. But the comforter can make an attractive wall-hanging, so if it comes with your set, you may still be able to use it.

Finally, a word about cosleeping (also sometimes called "the family bed"). Though cosleeping has gained in popularity in recent years, the American Academy of Pediatrics cautions against it (because it poses an increased risk of SIDS). Still, some pediatricians say it's OK, as long as you don't smoke or drink and you keep fluffy bedding away from the baby.

If you are certain that you want to cosleep with your baby, we recommend you purchase the Arms Reach Co-Sleeper or a similar cosleeping device. The cosleeper looks much like a play yard (and even converts to one) with one side lowered. It works like a bassinet, in that it enables the baby to sleep in a self-contained space (away from pillows and other suffocation hazards) right next to your bed. We like the convenience of a cosleeper because it enables us to be close to the baby for feedings and to check breathing (a common new-mommy compulsion) in the middle of the night. Still, if money is tight, a crib is a better investment, as the cosleepers can only be used until the baby can sit up or pull up.

2. ROCKING CHAIR

For some of us, the best part about having a baby is spending hours in a rocking chair, feeding, reading, and just comforting her. When shopping for a rocker, our most important advice is to try before you buy. Most of us love the glider rockers, but not everyone finds them comfortable. And what may be comfortable during pregnancy may not be comfortable once the baby is born. So, if at all possible, test out the rocker/recliner early in your pregnancy before you have a huge belly. How does your back feel? What about your arms? Try it with a baby doll to see how your arms fit on the rocker while feeding a baby. Consider, too, how your spouse/partner fits in the rocker. He'll be feeding, snuggling with, or reading to the baby, too, so he should also be comfortable.

Today's rocker recliners have everything from the capability of swiveling to built-in vibrating massagers.

Consider how and where you'll be using your rocker to see if these features are worth it. Most of us like the swivel feature, for example, because it lets us easily turn to reach a glass of water or put down a bottle on a table next to us.

If money is tight, you can skip the fancy ottoman and just get a cheaper wooden footstool or nursing stool.

You should also look ahead a few years when selecting a fabric. Consider what you'll do with the glider when your baby gets older. Will you have another baby and move it to his room? Will you sell it? Will you move it to the living room or den? Will you let your baby keep it in her room as she grows? Remember, you'll still be reading to your child long after he weans himself from the breast or bottle, so choosing a fabric that can stay in your child's room, but won't look unmistakably baby, is a great idea.

Another good idea is to get a rocker with slipcovers, so you can choose one to match your nursery, then change the slipcover if you want to move it to another room.

"A rocking chair is a must-have for your baby's room. You'll be spending a lot of time in it, so make sure it's comfortable. I recommend Dutalier gliders and ottomans. The glider reclines, rocks, and can be locked so it doesn't move. It also has pockets on either side for magazines, burp clothes, tissues, etc. The ottoman has a piece that slides out, so you can rest your feet while nursing. This also puts them at the perfect height. In addition, the ottoman glides with the glider. Well worth the money!"
—Katie Kroll, Smyrna, GA

"A rocking chair is great for nursing, soothing a crying baby, and reading bedtime stories. We got an upholstered one from Eddie Bauer that we can move into our living room when the baby gets older. It also has a washable slipcover, which is very important for a house with a new baby."
—Angela Anderson, Seattle, WA

"A rocking chair is a must. Get one that is comfortable. I like the ones with a bigger seat, so you have room to move around and reposition and tuck your legs under if you want. Make sure the arms are at the right height, so you can rest them when holding a baby. Also, test it out by leaning back and rocking with your feet, because this will be the position you find yourself in the most, holding a baby in your arms, rocking them to sleep."
—Dodi Kingsfield, Forestville, NY

"You can have the rocker in the baby's room or somewhere else in the house. The baby's room can get crowded with a rocking chair, so putting one in the master bedroom or living area can work okay, too. And the rocking chair will get more use and can be used for longer if it matches the house, rather than the baby's room."
—Kari Rydell, Ladera Ranch, CA

3. CHANGING TABLE

Some parenting books caution against buying a changing table. They say they are a waste of money, because they are only used for a few months and, most of the time, you end up changing the baby on a bed or the floor anyway. We couldn't disagree more. Unless you are very petite, changing a baby on a bed or the floor is uncomfortable. What's more, by the time the baby is old enough to crawl and walk, she is much more likely to try to squirm away on a bed or the floor than she is on a changing table.

We do recognize, however, that many changing tables are inadequate and poorly designed. Though they look nice, the changing table/dresser combinations are typically shorter in length than stand-alone changing tables, making their use shorter-lived. A stand-alone changing table with shelves or drawers underneath will last until your baby has outgrown diapers.

That's not to say these stand-alone models are designed perfectly, though. When will someone in the baby manufacturing world realize that we need enough space on the top of the changing table to put wipes, the old diaper, a new diaper, and the baby all at the same time? Sure, you can store wipes and diapers for future use on a shelf underneath the changing space. But when you're in the middle of changing a really messy diaper, you need to have a place to put the dirty diaper while you're still wiping the baby, and be able to reach for more wipes without having to bend underneath the table. It wouldn't hurt to have a spot for the fresh diaper on the same surface, either.

"I couldn't live without my changing table. It saved my back many times and allowed me to stay organized with all of the baby products."
—Holly Cocchiola, Bethlehem, CT

"It is important to have a good station for diapers. If you use a bed or the floor, you might end up with a sore back quickly. Get something high enough to make it comfortable for you. Also, make it comfortable for your baby and designate an area for all the supplies."
—Jennifer Rose, Ashland, MA

"Many people say a changing unit is a waste of money. Not for me. As a baby gift, my mother bought us a changing unit where the lid lifted up and there was a baby tub incorporated into the unit, and below that are drawers. This was great. I'm tall, and changing the baby on the bed, especially a preemie, which ours was the first time around, really hurt my back."
—Katie Anne Gustafsson, Eskilstuna, Sweden

4. DRESSER

You will need to have a place to put all those receiving blankets, onesies, and sleepers, and a dresser is the perfect choice. The style and brand is a matter of personal choice, but if money is tight, this is one item you can definitely borrow or buy secondhand. Check regular furniture stores for dressers, as they can be cheaper than juvenile furniture stores. But keep in mind if you go to a juvenile furniture store, you're more likely to find a dresser with childproofing features, such as drawers that are designed so kids' fingers can't being slammed in them.

It's nice to choose a dresser that matches your crib, but remember, the dresser can last a lifetime, while the crib will only be used for a few years, so choose something you'll want to live with for a while.

5. DIAPER PAIL

We're divided on the exact brand and style of diaper pail to buy, but we agree that you need a place to put diapers, and it should be kept close to where you regularly change the baby. Most of us shun the Diaper Genie ($24.95 at Babies R Us), because it can be hard to figure out how to use properly and a bit of a pain to change the bags. The Diaper Genie also requires special refill bags.

The newer Diaper Champ and Diaper Dekor promise to be easier to operate, while still controlling the smell. The Champ uses regular trash bags, and it is also less expensive than the Diaper Dekor ($29.95 compared to $39.95 at Babies R Us). However, the Dekor holds more diapers than both the Genie and the Champ, and allows for total hands-free operation.

We couldn't agree on an overall winner. Therefore, we recommend you try all three in a customer-friendly baby store, such as Buy Buy Baby, where the sales staff will help you experiment.

What Else to Buy

Other valuable items to have in your nursery include: a nightlight, lamp, night table, bookshelf, hamper, toy box, and a mobile. You won't need the nightlight for your baby; it's for you, so you can see his face when you go in to check on him. The lamp and night table come in handy for reading and providing a place to put bottles or water for you to drink while breastfeeding (breastfeeding will make you very thirsty).

You'll be shocked how many books and toys your baby acquires in an amazingly short period of time. It's relatively inexpensive to buy toys for kids this age, so relatives and friends can afford to be generous. It's nice to have a shelf on which to display your baby's toys, books, and stuffed animals. Hammocks also work well for stuffed animals and pretty baskets work well for books. If you do invest in a toy box, it won't be your last, but it's nice to have an attractive place to keep toys in the baby's room. It makes the room a place where you'll both want to spend time.

Make sure the mobile you choose faces the baby, so he can see it while lying in the crib. Most do nowadays, but some of the old-fashioned ones don't. Remember, babies can't see very far, and they prefer seeing black and white at first, so look for mobiles in those colors.

Finally, don't worry about getting everything you need right away. People will give you gifts for some months after the baby is born. And you'll also want some time to get to know your baby and see what both of you want and need.

Where to Buy It All

Shopping for your baby's nursery can be a blast, if you know where to look. Each of our three favorite spots gives you something different: One has the most attractive, pleasant atmosphere you can imagine. Our second choice has a huge selection. And our third has fabulous deals you can't get anywhere else. We recommend you try all three.

THE THREE BEST PLACES TO SHOP FOR BABY FURNITURE, WINDOW TREATMENTS, AND ACCESSORIES

1. Pottery Barn Kids (store, catalog, and website)
2. Babies R Us (store and website)
3. eBay

"Pottery Barn Kids has very cute and high-quality items. They also introduce new styles on a very frequent basis, so you can usually get what you want at sale or clearance prices when the new line is brought in."
—*Angela Anderson, Seattle, WA*

"I'm an eBay addict. I have found some great deals on gently used baby items. I got my son's entire crib bedding for under $30 there, and it looked brand new. You can find just about anything there . . . toys, clothes, bedding, nursery items, and more."
—*Veronica Wilson, Chattanooga, TN*

"Pottery Barn Kids has quality furniture and bedding that is very cute and not generic. They have different styles, depending on your taste. I also recommend eBay. You can find just about anything there for much cheaper than paying retail."
—*Eva Lindsey, Dallas, TX*

"Babies R Us is always good, especially if you want to try to do all your shopping in one place. It's not really overpriced, especially if you look for sale items."
—*Krisztina Rab, Naperville, IL*

"I love Pottery Barn Kids—such fun stuff for kids. I will find what I want to get through their catalog and then I will hop onto eBay and see if I can find it (new and in the package of course) for a cheaper price. So far, I have always found what I have been looking for."
—*Colleen Bouchard, Bel Air, MD*

CHAPTER THREE

Baby Gear

Perhaps the biggest shock to first-time moms (after the realization that your belly will eventually expand to a full forty inches) is the amount of baby equipment you'll need to buy. Heck, there are stores that do nothing but sell baby gear! Some of it is nice to have, some of it is a total waste of money, and some of it is absolutely essential. In this chapter, we'll help you discern which pieces of equipment fall into which category and show you how to save money on all of it.

Infant Car Seats

By now you probably know that infant car seats come in two varieties: the bucket kind that comes with a separate base; and the convertible car seat, which stays in the car and faces rear at first, then gets turned around to face forward once the baby is twenty pounds *and* at least one year old.

In general, we prefer the bucket-style infant car seats because they function as infant carriers, too, allowing you to pick the baby up and carry her wherever you're going. But your preference may depend on how big your baby is. For example, if you have a small- to average-sized baby, you will enjoy the convenience of a bucket-style infant car seat, because it allows you to move the baby in and out of the car without waking her. Bucket-style infant car seats also can be easily dropped into "travel systems" or lightweight stroller frames, which effectively turn the car seat into a stroller, again without waking the baby.

If you have a big baby, however, he may be too heavy to carry around in a bucket-style car seat for very long. Moreover, your big baby will likely outgrow this type of seat before the first year is up, and you may end up having to buy a convertible car seat anyway. (Remember, the baby has to be twenty pounds *and* at least one year old before you can turn him around to face forward, so if he hits twenty pounds at eight months, you need a car seat that can accommodate him facing backward.)

Though most of us are fans of the travel systems, which incorporate a bucket-style infant car seat into a stroller, many bucket-style infant car seats nowadays will fit into any full-sized stroller. So you don't necessarily have to buy a travel system in order to be able to move your sleeping baby from car seat to stroller and back without waking her.

A downside to the travel systems is that they are bulky. A good alternative is a lightweight stroller frame, such as the Kolcraft Universal Car Seat Carrier or the Snap-N-Go by Baby Trend, which works with all bucket-style infant car seats.

Of course, no matter what style infant car seat you choose, you should always choose one with a five-point harness. This is the safest.

Never buy a used car seat, such as from a yard sale. It may have been recalled or in an accident (you can't always tell), and car seats that have been in accidents should not be used again. If you want to save money and you're buying the bucket-style infant car seat, there's no need to buy another one for your second car. Simply purchase an additional base, and move the carrier part back and forth as needed.

Always have your car seat installed by a professional. Sure, you may take some flack from your brother-in-law who claims he moved his ten-year-old's car seat back and forth between cars all the time. What he didn't know is that he was risking her life in doing so, as an estimated 80 percent of car seats are installed incorrectly. This is not something to mess around with—we are talking about your baby's life!

Most cities can refer you to experts who have been trained in car seat installation (they must take a two-week course). If you live in the U.S., check out the National Highway Traffic Safety Administration's website (www.nhtsa.org) for referrals to experts in your state.

Finally, be sure to fill out the registration card that comes with your car seat. This is the only way you can be sure you'll be notified if there is ever a recall of your car seat.

OUR TOP PICK
FOR A BUCKET-STYLE INFANT CAR SEAT

Graco SnugRide

"I recommend a Graco car seat because any Graco car seat will snap into any other Graco carriage. When I have another baby, I can buy a Graco double stroller and know my infant seat will fit. Also, I had a minor problem with a Graco product and their customer service department was fantastic. Graco is also the only company so far that I know makes a running stroller with an infant car seat. I got this and then purchased another Graco stroller for under $100 to use as my primary stroller. I also found that they carried a lot of different patterns."
—Susan Dobratz, Plymouth, MA

"I really like the Graco SnugRide. It just seems to fit my baby better and is actually easier to get in and out of the car than the ones we had with our first two boys, because of the lever located at

the head of the seat. With the older ones, we had to move the handle back and forth to lock and unlock it."
—*Wendy Douglas, Margate, FL*

"For an infant seat, Graco is my personal favorite. Their seats are cost-effective, and Graco is a reputable company. The SnugRide is a great seat!"
—*Lamiel Oesterreicher, Brooklyn, NY*

OUR ABSOLUTE FAVORITE CONVERTIBLE CAR SEAT

Britax Roundabout

"The Britax Roundabout may be more expensive than some of the others, but it is well worth the price. Made in England, it exceeds all safety standards required in the U.S. It is made of a special material, which makes it superior in its ability to sustain the impact of a crash. It can be used for a wider range of weights— rear-facing, it can be used up to thirty pounds, whereas most car seats have a limit of twenty pounds; front-facing, it can be used from twenty to forty pounds. It also has a tether, and there are several cute fabric styles available."
—*Diane Bedrosian, M.D., Carlsbad, CA*

"I won't recommend any other car seat but the Britax. It is wonderful. It is expensive, but it's one that you will use for a long time. It can be used rear-facing and front-facing. It holds five to forty pounds. Also, the seat covers can be washed and come in great styles that can be changed. It has a pad between the child's legs that keeps the strap that goes there from burning the child when it's hot. And it has great head support. Britax is a wonderful brand."
—*Anna Maria Johnson, Shreveport, LA*

"I love Britax. I have everything from the newborn one through a toddler one that faces rear to a five-point harness that goes to eighty pounds and a wonderful, comfortable, easy-to-use booster that goes to one hundred pounds. Britax is the best brand. It is worth every penny."

—*Kate Hallberg, Boulder, CO*

Strollers

Do you ever plan to take a walk with your baby? Go to the park or a mall? Run errands that require a lot of walking? You will need a stroller.

And to find the right one for you, you need to consider what your primary use(s) for it will be. Will you use it mostly for walks to the park and trips to the mall? Jogging? Travel? Quick errands? There is a stroller made for each of these uses, and the features you'll want and need differ accordingly. Jogging strollers, for example, are terrific for going to the park, taking walks, and, of course, jogging. But they are too big for quick errands, and they'd be a royal pain to take on an airplane.

Full-size strollers are ideal for shopping and trips to the park and beach, but can be bulky to take in and out of the car when you're running errands and can take up too much room in the trunk to be left in the car all the time. Umbrella strollers are lightweight, but they have smaller wheels that handle poorly on long walks and trips to the park. Also, most umbrella strollers don't accommodate infants who can't sit up. Finally, lightweight stroller frames, in which the infant car seat doubles as the seat, are perfect for almost any trip with an infant, as long as you get one with a big basket, but they can only be used while the baby is in the infant car seat.

The fact is there is a very good chance you will end up owning more than one stroller. Just trust us on this. So we aren't going to discuss every possible stroller you could buy for every possible need. Instead, we'll focus on the first stroller.

OUR ABSOLUTE FAVORITE FIRST STROLLERS

1. Any brand of travel system (which includes a stand-alone stroller and a car seat that fit together).
2. A lightweight stroller frame, such as Kolcraft's Universal Car Seat Carrier or Baby Trend's Snap-N-Go, into which you snap an infant car seat.

"We did not have a snap-and-go for my first child, but I did buy one for my second. This was the best product I ever owned and a must-have for any new mom. We had the Kolcraft [Universal Carrier], which was great because it was easy to use, lightweight, and had a big basket and a cup holder/tray."
—Debbie Ezrin, Gaithersburg, MD

"We wanted a three-in-one type stroller, one that was rough and tumble and could go anywhere. The one we found has a base, into which you can snap the regular stroller seat, a carriage or pram-type bed, or the infant car seat. I love that it's so versatile. I just unhook the baby from the car and snap the car seat or carriage/car bed into the base. It's also great now that I have two, as I can easily change from the regular stroller for my two-year-old to the car seat for the baby."
—Cara Vincens, Thionville, France

THE TOP TEN FEATURES TO LOOK FOR WHEN SHOPPING FOR YOUR FIRST STROLLER

1. Light enough for you to lift in and out of your car
2. Big basket
3. Easy to open and close, preferably with one hand
4. A cup holder for the parents
5. Big wheels for "driving" on rough terrain or long walks
6. The ability to recline fully for infants who can't sit up
7. A cup holder for the baby
8. Easy maneuverability, preferably one-handed steering ability

9. Tray for the baby

10. The ability to reverse the direction baby faces (you vs. outward)

"Get something that doesn't weigh a ton and something that folds easily (ask to take it to your car to see how well it fits in your trunk—I did it, so don't laugh). If you plan to go walking or to the mall, get something that can hold your drink as well as the baby's and storage for the diaper bag is a must."
—*Anita Good, Hewitt, NJ*

"A big basket is the most important feature. Most people I know focus on weight, but that is not nearly as important as having enough room for a big diaper bag, your purse, shopping bags, coats, and all of the other junk that seems to end up down there."
—*Debbie Ezrin, Gaithersburg, MD*

"I would recommend a stroller with cup holders. If you are a nursing mother, you need to drink a lot of water and tend to be thirsty all the time. It helps to have handy access to a beverage while you take those walks. I took a lot of walks on varied terrain, and I liked a stroller with a lot of shock absorption. Of course, the sturdier the stroller, the heavier the stroller. If you are less likely to be walking around town and more likely to be lifting it in and out after car rides to the store, you might want a lightweight umbrella-style stroller."
—*Jennifer Rose, Ashland, MA*

"Check out the height of the stroller. Tall people (over 5' 8" or so) will find most brands are made for shorter people, and it really takes a toll on your back. MacLarens tend to be made for taller people. The stroller extensions available in catalogs are a total waste.

"Check the maneuverability of the stroller. You'll be turning lots of corners and dodging all sorts of obstacles, often with your hands full, so it's important to have wheels that turn easily."
—*Stacey Stevens, Alamo, CA*

"The most critical are: 1) lightweight, 2) easy to fold, 3) can steer with one hand, and 4) a basket large enough to hold your diaper bag and a shopping bag or two. Most mothers-to-be don't think about steering with one hand, but in about fifteen months, you will have a toddler who doesn't want to sit in the stroller. He wants to walk, and you need to hold his hand and push the stroller, too. Then a few months later, you need to be able to hold your older child's hand while pushing your newborn in the stroller. Many strollers are impossible to steer with one hand when they have weight in them."
—Tara Tucker, Mountain View, CA

"One of the biggest things for us was that we wanted the stroller to be able to recline fully, so that baby could lie flat. I thought that was important, but had no idea HOW important. For the first few months, it didn't make a difference, since she was in her infant carrier. Now, though, it is very nice to be able to let her nap in the stroller. Also, make sure you check how easy it is to adjust the seat position."
—Kris Taylor, Dallas, TX

High Chair

You don't have to buy a high chair before the baby is born, but you will eventually need a high chair or some sort of feeding chair when the baby starts to eat solid food. We look for a chair that is well-constructed (read: safe), reclines (baby probably won't be able to sit up straight at the first feedings), completely washable (leave the wood chairs in the antiques shops, please), and if space is a premium, can be stowed easily.

OUR TOP PICK (WARNING: IT'S PRICEY)

Peg Perego Prima Pappa

"I bought the Peg Perego Prima Pappa and am very happy so far. My daughter could be reclined in the beginning when she

was still bottlefeeding, and now that she is older, the chair has been great. It's very easy to use and grows with the child."
—*Angel Broussard, Lake Charles, LA*

"The Peg Perego Prima Pappa has several adjustments of height and also reclines. It is also easy to fold, so that it is completely portable."
—*Diane Bedrosian, M.D., Carlsbad, CA*

"My favorite brand is the Peg Perego Prima Pappa. The chair has three seat back positions, from fully reclined to fully sitting up. And it has seven height adjustments, so you can make sure the chair is at the right height for your table or counter or even your height for feeding. It has an easy-to-use tray that only requires one-hand operation and is very easy to clean."
—*Karen Hurst, Roseville, CA*

A GREAT INEXPENSIVE ALTERNATIVE

A portable booster seat, such as The First Years On-the-Go Booster Seat or the Safety First On-the-Go Fold-Up Booster Seat.

"The Safety First booster seat with attached tray is my only 'high chair.' I never purchased a high chair because we have a small kitchen, and I didn't want to take up the extra floor space with a chair that my children would outgrow in a matter of months. The booster chair comes apart easily for washing and can be folded for travel. I cannot recommend it highly enough, as a high chair substitute or as a toddler/preschooler booster."
—*Sidney Marks, Menlo Park, CA*

"I use the Safety Fisrt Portable 3-in-1 Booster Seat. It's inexpensive, and you can take it anywhere. Plus, some of the parts can be cleaned in the dishwasher."
—*Leah Chew, Tucker, GA*

"I actually returned my beautiful, but very impractical, wooden high chair because we liked this one (The First Years On-the-Go Booster) so much. The seat reclines to three different positions. Eventually, we can sit her at the table with no tray because it is attached to a chair. We have yet to find a chair it won't fit on . . . even our chair outside at the patio table. Both the seat and tray are dishwasher safe, the seat pad is super easy to take off and can be used with or without the pad, it's lightweight, and my three-year-old niece loves to sit in it when she is here. I like that it is able to grow so well with a child."

—*Susan Dobratz, Plymouth, MA*

Baby Products

There's no shortage of products on the market to make life easier for you and your little one. The trick is figuring out which ones are worth the money. Below are our top ten favorites, but keep in mind that baby gear is pretty subjective—what one mom considers a luxury, another might consider a necessity, depending on cost, lifestyle, and your baby's habits and preferences.

THE TEN BABY PRODUCTS YOU MUST HAVE

1. Swing
2. Bouncy seat (we recommend the Fisher-Price Ocean Wonders Aquarium Bouncer or the Fisher-Price Learning Patterns Infant to Toddler Rocker)
3. Boppy pillow
4. Cloth diapers or burp cloths
5. Baby Björn front carrier
6. Activity gym (we recommend the Gymini)
7. Sling (we recommend the Maya Wrap Sling)
8. Exersaucer
9. Monitor
10. Play yard (we recommend the Graco Pack 'N Play)

"You need enough props to have a 'station' in every usable room in the house. My must-haves are a swing in the kitchen, Exersaucer in the living room, floor gym in the baby's bedroom, and bouncy seat in the bathroom, so I can take a shower."
—*Jennifer Brannon, Huntington Beach, CA*

"I recommend the Fisher-Price Infant to Toddler Rocker (in the bouncy seat section). Our son loved sitting in this from the day we brought it home. Now he sits and watches TV, or mommy cook or whatever, in it. He has acid reflux, so it keeps him in a good position for sleeping. If he falls asleep, I just swing out the kick bar, and I never have to get him up."
—*Crystal Burriss, Raleigh, NC*

"The Boppy pillow is a great idea for every new mom. It can be used to support the baby while breastfeeding. Later, it can be used to prop the baby up during playtime, so she can play on her tummy. Then when the baby is sitting up, just that little bit of support behind her can save her from falling over."
—*Stephanie Smith, Alexandria, KY*

"I love the Baby Björn. I wish I had invented it. You really don't feel the weight of the baby on your back; somehow it really evenly distributes it."
—*Andrea Suissa, Olney, MD*

"I recommend a bassinet or a play yard that has a bassinet in it. The first few days of being home, it's nice to have a way for baby to sleep in your room. Plus, this can easily be set up in any room of the house and moved around as necessary, while the baby bed has to stay in place. Also, a bouncer is great. It's one of the few places you can safely sit baby during those first few months."
—*Amy Kobler, Buffalo, NY*

"If you find a good sling, you can use it for years. I know some moms that still use theirs occasionally with their four-year-olds.

You can go from cradle-hold to back-carry positions and everything in between.

"I recommend an unpadded one, such as the Maya Wrap or TaylorMade Treasure. Unpadded slings are better because they allow for more adjustability. For instance, you can adjust the top or bottom separately (something you can't do with a padded sling), allowing you to carry the baby on your back, if you like. Also, unpadded slings allow for more air circulation during the summer, keeping baby cooler."

—*Brenda Brown, Kapolei, HI*

"A Gymini activity gym is nice because it gives the newborn a change in position and lets them learn to reach and grab for objects. It's great entertainment!"

—*Jennifer Young, Bethesda, MD*

"New moms need a front carrier. I have a Baby Björn and really like it. When babies are little, they love the feeling of closeness and will go right to sleep. It's a way to get stuff done around the house or grocery shop while still holding your baby."

—*Katie Kroll, Smyrna, GA*

"A good-quality baby monitor and an Exersaucer came in handy for me when I needed to do laundry or take a shower (I had a baby who refused to nap until he was nine months old!). I also recommend lots of blankets and extra burp rags. You'll always have some clean that way."

—*Tessica Reynolds, Salt Lake City, UT*

"I recommend a Pack 'N Play. It's great to keep the little one contained and content. You can use it to store toys after the baby grows out of it. The one I had was a diaper changing table, a bassinet, and a playpen all in one. It's easy to travel with, if needed.

"I also recommend a swing. If your baby likes the swing, it can keep them occupied while you need to do some things around the house."

—*Judith Wu, Orange, CA*

AND FOUR PRODUCTS
THAT AREN'T WORTH THE MONEY

1. Diaper Genie
2. Wipe warmer
3. Bassinet (we recommend you borrow one, as it's used just a short time)
4. Fancy clothes

"The Diaper Genie is a big hassle to use and way too costly to keep refilling. In addition, it's often hard to find the replacements."
—*Valerie Downs, Altoona, PA*

"Avoid fancy, frilly clothes or anything without a snap crotch. You'll only use the fancy stuff for photos and it's more of a pain than anything."
—*Jennifer Brannon, Huntington Beach, CA*

"Avoid wipe warmers. They burn a lot of the wipes, and you can just use a warm washcloth instead. Also, buntings. They are cute, but not easy to put baby in. And stay away from footed sleepers that only snap at the bottom. They're too hard to get baby into and out of."
—*Kris Rivas, Denver, CO*

"Borrow or buy a bassinet or cradle from a consignment shop. Babies use them such a short time to spend a lot of money on them."
—*Anna Marie Menta, Clifton Heights, PA*

"Avoid fancy or complicated clothes. One-piece pajamas with zippers that are easy-on and easy-off are the best and easiest to deal with during middle-of-the-night diaper changes."
—*Angela Anderson, Seattle, WA*

What Else You Will Need

1. Receiving blankets (we recommend the Miracle Blanket)
2. Onesies
3. Sleepers and/or sleep sacks
4. Bulb syringe (for cleaning out baby's nose)
5. Baby bath tub or sling
6. Camera and/or camcorder
7. Diaper bag (we recommend Eddie Bauer brand)
8. Thermometer (see Chapter 13 for our favorite kind)

"I love, love, love my Eddie Bauer diaper bag. It is great as an infant diaper bag and when the baby grows up and you don't need to tote three changes of clothes around anymore, it does great as an overnight bag for stays at Grandma's house.

"It is stylish and not babyish, with its gray exterior. It has bottle pockets on either side, a zip-up compartment in the front and even has a key holder in there. The inside of the bag has a pocket strictly for the changing pad (included), a zip-up, heavy duty plastic insert to store dirty diapers or 'leakables' so everything doesn't get soiled or wet. And best of all, that compartment is removable. I can't brag enough about my Eddie Bauer bag."

—*Lamiel Oesterreicher, Brooklyn, NY*

"I recommend the Miracle Blanket for swaddling ease (www.miracleblanket.com). Swaddling helps soothe babies in so many ways, but mastering swaddling is next to impossible unless you're a nurse. My husband and I were shown countless times how to wrap our baby up like a little burrito, to no avail. The Miracle Blanket has a foot pouch and internal wraps so that it is easy to swaddle your baby, and more important, that baby stays swaddled."

—*Jennifer Brannon, Huntington Beach, CA*

"I had a lot of luck with my Eddie Bauer brand diaper bag. It has been worth the money, holds up well, and cleans up easily. I like the ones with many pockets, but are easily accessible, like with the cup holder on the side, and a cell phone pocket and a place for my wallet."

—*Kel Bright, Charleston, SC*

"Make sure your diaper bag is neutral or manly. You don't want daddy feeling embarrassed carrying around a bag with bunnies all over it. If he's embarrassed, he's less likely to offer to carry it! I loved my large and small Eddie Bauer navy diaper bags. They didn't scream diaper bag! You can even use them after you're done with diaper bags."

—*Carolyn Dunn, Morristown, NJ*

Baby Clothes

When we shop for baby clothes, we look for styles that will make diaper changes easy, especially when buying sleepers and pajamas. We recommend brands that will last through multiple washings and preferably, can be passed down to future children. And we generally recommend getting several different sizes at first, e.g., 0–3 months and 3–6 months, as babies outgrow clothes quickly, especially in the first six months.

You'll want to get several sleepers, side-snap T-shirts or onesies (undershirts that snap at the crotch), and lots of receiving blankets. These will be the mainstay of your baby's wardrobe at the beginning.

THE SIX BEST BRANDS OF BABY CLOTHES

1. Carter's
2. Old Navy
3. Baby Gap
4. Gymboree
5. Target Little Tykes (made by Carter's)
6. Lands' End

"I like Carter's. I have found that they run bigger than other brands, so the child is able to wear the clothes for a longer amount of time."
—*Tanya Rosario, Bronx, NY*

"I love Gap and Gymboree . . . clothes that last forever and return policies that are flexible. Oh yeah, and the sale prices are incredible. These stores can be found in most shopping malls, which is great if Grandma wants to buy something for her."
—*Chantal Laurin, Concord, Ontario, Canada*

"My favorite when my son was an infant was Carter's. I was determined not to purchase any clothing for our son with bears or sports themes, and Carter's offered lots of alternatives in bugs and other animals, as well as in the John Lennon collection.

"My other favorite is Old Navy. Again, the prices and style cannot be beat. But my absolute fave is Lands' End. Lands' End is a little pricey, but the clothing is well worth it."
—*Dana Croy, Murfreesboro, TN*

"I like Gymboree. I used to shop at Baby Gap, but after a while, I began to feel like I was dressing my baby like a preteen. I love Baby Gap for their quality, but wanted sweeter, more childlike designs. I sort of stumbled into Gymboree and was instantly in love with the designs and the quality. Gymboree has the softest and thickest cottons, outside of high-end children's shops. The prices are a little bit higher than Baby Gap, but they have frequent sales, and if you get on the Gymboree mailing list either through the website (www.gymboree.com) or your local store, you can receive invitations to special sales where the price really comes down. Gymboree also has a wonderful program called Gymbucks, where for every $50 you spend, you get $25 toward your next $50 purchase during redemption periods. Gymbucks runs several times a year, just in time for every season.

"If you can't afford Gymboree from the shop, there is a thriving eBay market where you can get really good-quality clothing for great prices."
—*Chaya Reich, Los Angeles, CA*

"Lands' End clothing is classically styled and very durable. The clothes are sized so that you can get more than one season out of them. My kids have been able to wear their Lands' End clothing for two or three years, and then hand them down to the next child who wears them for the same amount of time. They still look great even after all this wear."
—Julie Bartlett, Bettendorf, IA

"Gymboree clothes last much longer and hold up better than any other brand I have found."
—Keli Thakur, Fort Wayne, IN

"Target clothes are cheap and well-made. They are also stylish!"
—Tara Betteridge, Fort Lewis, WA

"I like Old Navy. My kids are very big, since their father is 6'4", so it is difficult to find clothes that are long enough, but Old Navy's clothes fit perfectly, hold up very well, and are reasonably priced."
—Eva Lindsey, Dallas, TX

Where to Get Baby Gear

Whether you're pregnant or you've already had the baby, your criteria for what makes a good shopping experience will be different from what you looked for before you got pregnant. Now, you'll want stores that are easily accessible. If you can't get there, shop, and be back in time for the baby's afternoon nap, it's too far. And if you're pregnant, who wants to schlep out of your way when you're carrying an extra twenty-five to forty pounds around?

Selection is important—not just because we like having choices, but because we don't have the time or energy to drive all around town to different stores to get what we need.

And prices better be competitive. This stuff doesn't come cheap. It doesn't hurt if we can get other shopping done at the same time. Any store that offers a good selection of baby products, plus other household necessities is invariably more attractive to us, since we can't buzz in and out of stores as easily as we used to anymore.

OUR THREE FAVORITE STORES FOR BABY PRODUCTS

1. Babies R Us
2. Target
3. Wal-Mart

"I shop at Wal-Mart and Target. They have great quality products at low prices. Baby clothes at Wal-Mart come at the best prices, even into the toddler years."
—Lisa McDonald, Maitland, FL

"I registered at Babies R Us right after I found out the sex of my baby, and I was amazed at the selection of baby products all in one place. The last thing I wanted to do at nine months pregnant was travel to different stores, and Babies R Us carried everything from bottles to bathtubs, furniture to books. The sales associates were always extremely helpful, and most of their items, such as strollers, are on display and available to 'test drive.'"
—Billie Smith, Turpin, OK

"My favorite store right now is Target. I shop at Target for baby products, toys, kids' clothes, etc. The reason I love Target so much is that I can get everything I need in one stop. Target generally has a good selection of items in stock at the right price. I appreciate the fact that I don't have to drive all over town to find things, and the 90-day return policy is great."
—Sidney Marks, Menlo Park, CA

Shopping Online

Time-crunched and sleep-deprived moms (wait a minute—doesn't that include *all* moms?) love shopping online because it gives us access to all the most creative and unusual baby products, plus the ability to shop from home at any time of the day or night, not to mention great prices (in many cases), and the ability to hop from store to store within minutes to find the best deals.

THE BEST WEBSITE FOR BABY PRODUCTS

BabyCenter.com

"BabyCenter.com has a great selection, good prices, lots of sales, free shipping promotions and no sales tax."
—*Angela Anderson, Seattle, WA*

"I love BabyCenter. Not only do they have a store with tons of items for sale, but they also have bulletin boards where moms can post questions to other moms with babies who are born in the same month and year. It has been wonderful when discussing such issues as breastfeeding, table foods, teeth, ear infections, and many milestones."
—*Stephanie Smith, Alexandria, KY*

"BabyCenter's selection and pricing are good, and the service is quick and reliable. The information available on the site is extremely helpful and the chat rooms are nice, too. My older son was born in 1996 before the dot.com explosion and before BabyCenter existed. I had many different pregnancy/baby books taking up space on my shelves and ran around to many different stores shopping for baby gear. When my second son was born in the summer of 1999, I found that I could get all the information I wanted and all the gear, too, from BabyCenter. Furthermore, I could shop online at times like 2 a.m., after a nighttime feeding, when all was quiet and I had no other family demands."
—*Susan Tachna, Palo Alto, CA*

CHAPTER FOUR

DELIVERY AND BEYOND

T he last trimester of pregnancy is a little like being the only woman on a ship of sailors who've been at sea for a long time: People are insanely attracted to you. Unfortunately, they're not really interested in learning about you. They're really interested in forcing you to listen to all the sordid details of their own labors and deliveries, down to the size of their episiotomies and the nasty names they called their partners during labor.

And if that isn't enough to annoy you to no end, then they'll start peppering you with questions that are absolutely none of their business, but which they still seem to feel no shame in asking. Questions such as, "Are you planning to have natural childbirth?" "Who's going to be in the delivery room with you?" And my personal favorite, "Are you videotaping the event, and when can I see it?" Run—don't walk—to the nearest exit when you hear that one!

The important thing to remember is to pay absolutely no attention whatsoever to what these meddling mothers have to say and to only listen to us, the meddling mothers whom you've paid good money to listen to.

We understand you may have some questions as you start to approach your due date. Questions like, "Gee, I wonder how this baby is going to get out of me anyway?" And "Natural childbirth sounds wonderful, but is there any way I can get just a little something, like a touch of morphine or a fifth of vodka, just to take the edge off during labor?" These are best posed to a licensed health care professional, like a doctor or midwife. (Just kidding on the morphine and vodka. But if it's comforting, there's nothing stopping you from *thinking* about it while you're in the throes of labor.)

Let's turn our attention to what we mommies know best: helping you get prepared for the big day, managing the transition to life with a new baby, and that ever-important subject of losing the pregnancy weight.

Preparing for the Big Day

TEN LOW-STRESS WAYS
TO GET READY FOR LABOR AND DELIVERY

1. Watch birthing shows on television.
2. Take prepared childbirth classes.
3. Read books about labor and delivery.
4. Make a birth plan, but be flexible. Realize that your ultimate goal is a healthy baby, not having everything go exactly according to plan.
5. Get organized: Pay bills in advance. Make plans for the care of your other kids and/or pets while you're in labor. Prepare meals you can freeze and use later. And have help lined up for when you get home, whether it's your mother, a friend, or a baby nurse or doula.
6. Pack a bag.
7. Join an online community of other expecting moms.
8. Tour the hospital or birthing center.
9. Decide who you want in the labor room and visiting in the hospital in advance, and make those wishes known to your family and the hospital or birthing center staff.
10. Plan to let the nurses take the baby for a while during your hospital stay.

"I hadn't been around hospitals much, let alone in the delivery room, so watching these births on TV, becoming familiar with the order of things, and seeing how hospitals operate really helped me. Some people say that you will scare yourself in that you'll see all the bad things that can happen when delivering a baby, but on the other hand, you see that in almost every delivery emergency, everything turns out okay.

"I was certainly more relaxed during my epidural administration, for example, because I had seen it done so many times on TV. The real procedure was much less scary than what I was envisioning in my head during the labor and delivery classes."
—*Amy Kubecka, Palacios, TX*

"Before the baby gets here, cook meals and freeze them. That way, all you need to do is take them out and put them in the microwave."
—*Ange Gregory, Stanwood, IA*

"Take a tour of the hospital or birthing center before you deliver. Get familiar with how things are set up and run, and meet the staff. It will make you feel more comfortable and relaxed when the big day comes."
—*Dianna Schisser, Frederick, MD*

"BabyCenter has a great bulletin board system that groups expecting moms by the month of their due date. In this community, I was able to read about other moms who were going through the exact same things I was, and when it came time for our babies to be born, I got to read about the experiences of the moms who gave birth before I did."
—*Brandi Leach, Fort Worth, TX*

"I think it is very important not to have high expectations for wanting delivery to go a certain way. There are too many unknowns about what could/will happen for you to think things have to go a certain way. I would try to be open-minded about what can happen, so you aren't disappointed in the results."
—*Jana Bell, London, OH*

"I felt the delivery was a personal moment between me and my husband. My parents and mother-in-law were in the waiting room, but the delivery room was off-limits. But after the baby was born, I actually preferred visitors in the hospital, not at home. In the hospital, the visit is limited. This made it easier than having guests who didn't leave or whom you have to entertain. And I didn't have to try to pick up my house."
—Amy Kobler, Buffalo, NY

"Accept that things rarely go according to plan and that the most important part is that the baby is delivered safely into the world. After all, you tell people where you have been on holiday, but rarely is the mode of transport mentioned! Delivery might not be the way you've dreamed about it for months or even the way that the pregnancy book, Lamaze class, or your friends tell you it 'ought to be,' but that doesn't matter. Pain doesn't make you bond with your baby; love does."
—Katie Anne Gustafsson, Eskilstuna, Sweden

"I had relatives there one hour after delivery. Never again. It was too much, and I never really got to spend quality time right after the birth with just me, hubby, and the baby. If you have a family who just can't take no for an answer, I suggest that when you get to the hospital, tell the nurses no visitors until I say so. That way, you can blame it on hospital policy."
—Holly Cocchiola, Bethlehem, CT

"Let the nurses take the baby once in a while. You'll never have that luxury again. I wanted my son with me the entire time in the hospital, and I didn't get any sleep. I think it was a good three months into motherhood before I got a good night's rest."
—Karen Cutchin, Portland, ME

What to Bring to the Hospital

Books and prenatal childbirth classes are famous for coming up with long lists of items to bring to the hospital. We found some of these suggestions to be helpful, but many of these items never got used, (really, does anybody use those tennis balls?) while other, critical items were left out. Here's what we think are the most crucial items to pack in your hospital bag.

THE TEN MOST IMPORTANT THINGS TO BRING TO THE HOSPITAL WHEN YOU'RE READY TO DELIVER

1. Camera (and film if it's not digital)
2. Robe, comfortable nightgown, or pajamas with easy access to your breasts, if nursing
3. Your personal phone book and calling cards
4. Socks or slippers
5. Car seat for the baby
6. Pillow from home
7. Nursing bra
8. Snacks
9. Makeup
10. The baby's father!

"My second delivery took forever because it was induced, and it was very helpful that I brought along my telephone book because I was able to hand it off to a family member so they could call important people to let them know what was going on."
—April McConnell, Birdsboro, PA

"Bring your own pillow. The ones at the hospital are really flat!"
—Tara Betteridge, Fort Lewis, WA

"Warm socks and makeup! The socks are nice to have on during labor and delivery because hospital rooms are notoriously cold. And the makeup will help mom feel human again after giving birth—at least it did for me. It's nice to look back at all the pictures of me with our baby and NOT want to cut my own face out of the photo."
—Tracy Pritchard, Kyle, TX

"Most important to me that no one warned me about: calling cards since most hospitals don't allow cell phones to be used."
—Amy Kubecka, Palacios, TX

"Don't forget your makeup! Sounds shallow, but I felt much better after I was able to put on a little mascara and lipstick."
—Daryl D'Angelo, Sewell, New Jersey

"Make sure you bring along some snacks for Dad. You will probably be laboring at some point during the night when the hospital cafeteria may be closed, and there are just vending machines to get snacks from. We took a small cooler and filled it with easy-to-eat things like Lunchables for my husband to eat while I was in labor. By doing this, it meant that he never had to leave my side during the whole process."
—Brandi Leach, Fort Worth, TX

"The father. No kidding! I had to drive myself to the hospital in labor while my husband finished out his workday. He wanted to make sure it was time before he took off from work. I was walking the halls for two hours, lugging my bag, trying to coax my cervix along before they would admit me, alone. I have never forgiven him for that! Make sure your spouse has his priorities straight."
—Diana Molavi, M.D., Baltimore, MD

Your Wardrobe After the Baby Is Born

When you're pregnant for the first time, you often fantasize about getting back into your regular clothes after the baby is born. But once you've had one child, you know those skinny jeans don't just glide on moments after giving birth. Here are our recommendations for those first few months after the baby comes.

THREE KEY RULES FOR YOUR NEW MOMMY WARDROBE

1. Comfort is key.

2. Get tops that allow easy access to your breasts if you're nursing.

3. Keep the maternity clothes, but if wearing them bothers you, buy new clothes in larger sizes until you lose the weight.

"For me, all three times after delivery, the skin on my belly was very sensitive the first week after delivery, and the most comfortable clothes were loose-fitting clothes, like dresses and very stretchy underwear."
—*Barbara Nichols, Okeechobee, FL*

"I found that buying pants with Lycra (stretch) is good for when you want to start wearing real clothes, but you are not yet down to your prepregnancy weight. Lands' End has washable stretch pants that work great. My favorite pants with stretch are the Halogen and Classiques Entier brands at Nordstrom. They have high waists and stretch to make the fit comfortable, but look good. They are great for when you are first pregnant and after the baby when you have not quite returned to your prepregnancy weight. And they last, which is important."
—*Beth Blecherman, Menlo Park, CA*

"Be realistic. Keep out the maternity clothes and some larger, loose-fitting clothes—anything that is comfortable."
—*Heather Hendrickson, Yucaipa, CA*

"Don't feel guilty or bad that you have to wear maternity clothes for a while after. It's better to be comfortable in these than miserable trying to squish yourself into your favorite jeans. It took me eight months before I could get into my jeans and another month before they looked good."
—*Cara Vincens, Thionville, France*

"I think nursing gowns are for the birds, same with the shirts. They don't work very well. Snap-up shirts are the best for nursing because they are easy to get out of in a hurry (and believe me, you hurry when you have a screaming, hungry baby on your hands!). Next best are T-shirts—big ones. I still wore my maternity T-shirts long after I had the baby, because they gave me the room to pull them up and feed the baby."

—*Heather Meininger, Charlotte, NC*

Now About Those Extra Pounds

Once the initial cocooning period has passed—you're getting showers on a regular basis, you get dressed every day (or at least most days), and the aches and pains of delivery have healed—you may be ready to think about how you're going to get back into your prepregnancy clothes.

NOTE: If you got into your skinny jeans two weeks after delivery, please keep that milestone to yourself. We have fragile egos, not to mention wild hormonal swings in these first months after having a baby, and we prefer not to torture ourselves with stories of women whose pregnancy weight melted off them with less effort than a lick of a (nonfat) ice cream cone. Here are the best ways to battle the post-pregnancy bulge and win.

THE FOUR EASIEST WAYS TO LOSE THE PREGNANCY WEIGHT

1. Breastfeed
2. Exercise
3. Eat right
4. Give yourself time

"I have to believe that breastfeeding is the best way to lose the weight. It certainly contracts your uterus, and that helps you look better and fit into your pants quicker. You can experience

the joy of eating more than you did when pregnant and still lose weight!"
—*Jennifer Rose, Ashland, MA*

"Without a doubt, jogging is the easiest and fastest way to lose weight after having a baby. You don't have to learn a new skill (you learned that as a toddler!), and you don't have to join a gym."
—*Angela Snodgrass, Meridian, ID*

"Breastfeeding naturally uses calories, plus, it causes the uterus to contract, which makes it go back to its natural shape faster. Three weeks after I had my first baby, I lost 28 pounds! I had gained 65, I might add, but it still felt great to lose that much so fast."
—*Dayna Lawson Gilmore, The Woodlands, TX*

"Weightwatchers.com. Memorize it. Use it. It works. I was almost into a size 18. (Okay, I was a size 18 and was disgusted.) Ellie was 15 months old, and I was 20 pounds away from a size 14 (I'm 6 feet tall). I ran into another doctor mom at the hospital who had clearly recently lost a ton of weight and who looked, well, phenomenal. I asked her what she had done and how she had found the time. 'Weight Watchers Online' was her reply. 'It's cheaper [than joining in person], and if you're self-motivated like I am, it works.' Go for it gals. I've lost it and kept it off for six months now."
—*Michele Carlon, M.D., Chicago, IL*

Coming Home

Those first weeks and months after having a baby are filled with emotion—abundant love for this sweet little newborn, combined with hair-pulling exhaustion and often, bouts of depression. Many of us focus exclusively on the baby's needs, often to the detriment of our own. Paradoxically, however, the best thing you can do for the baby as well as yourself, is to put your own needs front and center. Here are our best ideas for making the transition to life with a new baby easier.

OUR SEVEN-STEP PLAN FOR A SUPER EASY TRANSITION TO LIFE WITH A NEW BABY

1. Limit visitors in the first few weeks, especially those who expect to be treated as guests.
2. Accept help.
3. Make sleep a top priority. Get rest whenever and wherever you can.
4. Encourage and accept the new dad's help and involvement.
5. Let the house go.
6. Get organized in advance.
7. Do something nice for yourself every day.

"I remember my first day home from the hospital, all I wanted to do was sleep and bond with my new little friend. And yet, people continued to drop by unannounced wanting to hold the baby and take our pictures. It was so frustrating. We finally decided to make a sign for the door that said, 'Mommy and Brendan are sleeping. Come back later.' I know that may seem cold, but it was our last resort for peace and quiet."
—*Katie Conroy, Palos Hills, IL*

"Don't ever be afraid to ask for help. Don't feel like you need to be a superwoman and single-handedly cook, clean, care for the baby, care for all your other family members, pay the bills, etc. There should be no guilty feelings about being human and needing help. Many people are delighted to have something to do, so they feel useful, even if it's laundry or dishes."
—*Krystal Johnston, M.D., Manistee, MI*

"Don't get upset when things are rough in the beginning. I felt like a bumbling idiot, but I remembered a line from a poem that our birthing instructor gave us. It reminds us new parents that our little one doesn't realize that we messed something up, because they are new at being a baby."
—*Melissa Best, Avella, PA*

"Repeat after me, 'My doctor recommends I have as few visitors as possible in the first two weeks.'"
—*Donnica L. Moore, M.D., Branchburg, NJ*

"Get a nanny! Let others help for at least the first two weeks."
—*Dayna Lawson Gilmore, The Woodlands, TX*

"With my first baby, I thought I could do everything myself. With the birth of my twins, I had a list of things I needed to get done, and anytime someone asked if they could help, I said, 'Here is the list. Pick something and let me know when you'll be coming over to do it.'

"I also tried to make and freeze as many meals in advance as I could. It was much easier to defrost something than try to cook a meal. Let it be known to all your friends and neighbors that a gift for the baby is nice, but the best gift that I got from my neighbors was a basket full of gift certificates to places that deliver!"
—*Daryl D'Angelo, Sewell, NJ*

"If I had to do it all over, I'd ask for shorter visits, and, instead of more tiny outfits, I'd ask for a casserole shower. That is when friends and family make you freezable dinners so you don't have to worry about cooking after delivery."
—*Carolyn Dunn, Morristown, NJ*

"Give the new dad plenty of responsibility in caring for your baby. While you may feel possessive now, the time will come when you will want and need the help, and if dad doesn't learn how to help now, he won't be equipped when you really need him later. Plus, you want your baby to have the strongest possible bond with dad, and this is how it starts."
—*Theresa Smead, St. Louis, MO*

"Number one rule: Don't be a martyr! When people ask what they can do, don't ever say, 'I don't know,' or 'We're okay.' If you don't accept the offers, they'll quit asking. And don't be vague. Have specific tasks in mind. Here were some that we found very useful for us:

Have them bake ready-to-heat dinners for your freezer.

Send them to the grocery/drugstore with a blank check and a shopping list.

Have them address envelopes for birth announcements and/or thank-you notes.

Have them make announcement phone calls.

Have them clean your house/do laundry/wash dishes/mow the lawn.

Have them rent movies or check out reserved library books for you.

"Number two: You are the mommy. You decide when visitors arrive and how long they stay. You are not obligated to entertain or serve snacks when people come by, and it is your prerogative to tell family friends, 'This isn't a good time. Can you come by later?'

"We left a note taped over our doorbell that thanked people for their kindness/concern, etc., and asked that if they had any deliveries to please leave them at the doorstep. Our twins spent a LONG stretch in the Neonatal Intensive Care Unit, so we also left a message on our answering machine that gave a brief update of the boys' condition and an apology that we would likely be unable to return all of the phone calls we received. This really cut down on the forty-five 'How are they doing?' messages we got at the end of the day."

—*Jenna Haldeman, Portland, OR*

CHAPTER FIVE

Birth Announcements, Baby Namings, and Baptisms, Oh My!

You've finally met your little one; now you want the whole world to know she's arrived! How do you spread the news? Immediate family and close friends will undoubtedly get a phone call hours (maybe even moments) after birth. But you may also want to do something religious, fun, or more formal to share the milestone with your whole circle of friends and relatives.

We've seen everything from traditional printed birth announcements to personalized fortune cookies announcing baby's arrival. And celebrations can range from christenings for just the immediate family to catered baptisms for two hundred. Whatever route you choose to announce and celebrate your baby's birth, we're here to help you make it the easiest, and most special, possible.

The Eight Most Creative Ways to Announce Your Baby's Birth

1. Baby website
2. E-mail with a link to the hospital web page

3. Custom fortune cookies

4. Custom beer

5. DVD of the baby's first pictures

6. Announcement that looks like a newspaper article

7. Message on your car or house or wooden stork in your front yard

8. Custom candy bars

"You can make a web page on babiesonline.com. It's free, easy, they have adorable setups and this allows you not only to announce baby, but show him/her off! What better way to let relatives out of town see the baby!"
—*Kelly Harden, Fort Hood, TX*

"Microbreweries are very big in Seattle, and there are a few places where you can make and bottle your own beer with a custom label, which, of course, could replace the traditional cigar as a baby announcement. A lot of people in this area use e-mail and custom websites as well."
—*Angela Anderson, Seattle, WA*

"A friend of mine sent out DVDs with some of the baby's first pictures put to music on it. It was lovely and a wonderful way to share their experience with those of us closest to her."
—*Brooke Kuhns, Dayton, OH*

"The easiest way I have seen is to send an e-mail with a link to the hospital web page. It seems most larger hospitals are now providing that service, and you can see the first photo of the baby immediately (and no getting stamps, addressing envelopes, and writing nice little unique notes on announcements)."
—*Sarah Fox, Fort Collins, CO*

"There's a place called Creative Fortune Cookies that will make fortune cookies with the baby's info inside. Then you can send them to friends. I thought that was a cute idea.

"My husband is a textbook rep, and had business cards

made up announcing his company's 'Newest Supplement.' He handed those out to business associates."
—*Kris Taylor, Dallas, TX*

EDITOR'S NOTE: You can order custom fortune cookies online from Products with Personality (www.pwponline.com) and Fancy Fortune Cookies (www.fancyfortunecookies .com).

"The most creative way I've heard of a baby being announced was a card that looked like a newspaper article with the picture in it."
—*Michele Carlon, M.D., Chicago, IL*

EDITOR'S NOTE: Proud Parent Publications (www.proud parentpublications.com; 414-421-7007) creates humorous birth announcements that are designed to look like newspaper or magazine stories. Styles range from *Baby Today*, designed to look like *USA Today*, to *It's About Time*, designed to look like *Time* magazine. Proud Parent writes the article; you simply submit the vital statistics. Story themes include presidential election, world premiere, baseball, beauty pageant, and more.

"I like the idea of a message on the car, a banner on the new mommy's house, or a welcome baby ad in the local paper. On the car, everyone driving by can see it. And on the house, it is a welcome home for mommy and baby (makes mom feel good that people care), and neighbors will know and maybe a couple of neighbors will bring over food and stuff to help mommy out on her first days home with the new baby."
—*Dafni Mauchley, Phelan, CA*

"Having family far away, I love the websites like www.growth spurts.com or www.babiesonline.com. I also liked the idea a family I knew had. They used fabric paint to write the stats on a onesie, then took a picture of the baby in it and sent it out. It seemed so much more personal."
—*Brenda Brown, Kapolei, HI*

"A friend had her announcements put on candy wrappers, and I just thought it was really a unique way of making an announcement. I found this website for candy wrapper announcements (www.candy-bar-wrappers.com) and had no idea all this existed!"
—*Bobbi Annal, Spokane, WA*

The Five Easiest Ways to Get Your Birth Announcements Done Fast

1. Preorder announcements and address and stamp the envelopes before birth.
2. Do them on your computer.
3. Order photo announcements online.
4. Send out an e-mail with a photo of the baby.
5. Use the hospital's birth announcement service.

"You can order them before the baby is born, then call the company to fill in the specifics of date, time, weight, etc., if you like. Then you can mail the announcements when you get them. I asked the company to send me the envelopes ahead of time, so I could have them addressed and stamped before the baby arrived. That way, I or a friend, could stuff them and mail them. Simple and easy."
—*Kerith Leffler, Morristown, NJ*

"The easiest is a photo announcement from an online company. You send them your photo (digital or film), use their website to choose a card design and pay for it, and they mail them to you. Some, like Ofoto.com, will even mail them out for you."
—*Shelly Knight, Longmont, CO*

"While the professionally printed baby announcements are lovely, they can also be quite expensive. We just didn't have it in our budget, so we created our own. With a decent computer design program, a printer, a digital camera, and some card stock, it can be an easy and inexpensive way to tell the world your good news. Our cards featured our daughter's tiny little feet. The

cards were personalized and definitely from the heart—and we got so many wonderful comments!"
—*Elizabeth Hildebrand, Greenville, PA*

"I have a friend who just had a baby, and she got birth announcements from Sam's Club. She did it all online. She just uploaded the pictures from her computer to Samsclub.com, then picked out what style she wanted, and they sent them to her a few days later."
—*Keli Loveland, Bartlett, TN*

"An e-mail with a picture of the baby makes a great first announcement. It's quick, easy, and everyone gets to hear the news right away."
—*Jennifer Weintraub, Dallas, TX*

"I always do an initial announcement via e-mail and post pictures online right after, then send a formal announcement later, after we have all settled home for a while."
—*Kari Rydell, Ladera Ranch, CA*

"Take advantage of the service provided to you at the hospital. All of the hospitals I have been in come around with a little package where you can order announcements while you are still there, and you can pay before you leave the hospital. That way, it's taken care of, you don't have to worry about it when you get home, and the announcements come in a variety of options. They come to your home in the mail in a relatively short period of time."
—*Dodi Kingsfield, Forestville, NY*

Secrets for Planning a Stress-Free Baptism, Bris, Baby Naming, or Christening

1. Do as much as possible in advance.
2. Delegate, delegate, delegate.
3. Have it at a restaurant or someone else's house.
4. Have it catered or have others bring food.
5. Keep it small and simple.

"Cater the food and hire someone to serve/replenish platters and clean up. Without hiring someone, I wouldn't have enjoyed the party. I used Eatzi's to cater, and the food was delicious, pretty, and reasonably priced. Platters came with black plasticware and napkins, which meant one less detail for me to worry about.

"Let your brother-in-law off the hook in attending the religious ceremony by having him set up the house and let the caterer in. Minimize decorations. We just used some fresh flowers in little clear bowls that I bought at the dollar store, and they looked great. Have toys available so kids attending have something to do besides run around."

—*Marlo Greenspan, Boyds, MD*

"Have someone else do most of the arranging for you! We wanted our firstborn christened in the UK and so other than phoning the reverend to arrange a date, sending out the invitations, and having an 'interview' with the reverend, my family over there organized everything, from the shopping of Jake's christening clothes to the reception afterwards, including catering and decorations! My mum and sister asked what kinds of things I'd like and talked with me about options, but they dealt with the organizing and coordinating, even on the day itself which meant we were able to enjoy our baby's special day without worrying if things were going okay."

—*Katie Anne Gustafsson, Eskilstuna, Sweden*

"Make sure you have a parent or friend in charge of greeting guests, showing them where to place presents, and showing them where the ceremony will take place. Also, that same person can make the calls to let friends and family know where the ceremony will be and when. Talk with the person performing the ceremony and get a list of the necessary items beforehand. That way, you can have them on hand. For example, for a bris, you'll need a yarmulke for the baby, vaseline, gauze pads, the parents' and baby's Hebrew names, etc."

—*Robyn Greenhouse, Gaithersburg, MD*

"I had the baptisms out or catered, which made life a lot easier for me. Also, let people help! My kids' godmother wanted to buy the baptism outfits. I let her, and it's a beautiful remembrance of their godmother."
—*Amy Kobler, Buffalo, NY*

"Have the reception at someone else's home. That way, the new mom doesn't have to clean on top of everything else."
—*Kris Rivas, Denver, CO*

The Simple Four-Step, No-Hassle Plan for Getting Thank-You Notes Done Fast

Having a baby is a little like having your own special holiday. Even if you don't send birth announcements or never have a religious ceremony to celebrate the baby's birth, people will just automatically lavish gifts on you. It's really quite nice! The bad news is gifts mean thank-you notes. And while you, no doubt, truly want to express your gratitude to the people who've taken the time to think of you, how do you find the time? Never fear. With our four-step plan, you'll have your thank-you notes done in no time!

1. Stock up on supplies (notes, envelopes, stamps, etc.) in advance.
2. Do them right away, so you don't have them hanging over your head.
3. Break the task down into manageable chunks; set a goal of accomplishing a certain number of notes per day.
4. Get help (have someone address them, have your husband write them, dictate what you want to say to a visitor and have her write them, etc.).

"Order thank-you cards at the same time as your announcements (if you already picked an announcement you like, you probably will like the thank-you card without spending any time searching for one). Order a lot (I think I got three hundred), because not only do you use them for baby's 'welcome' gifts, but also for baby naming/christening gifts, first birthday gifts, and everything in between.

"Write them immediately when you open the gift, so they don't pile up—it's easier to write three during baby's nap, than twenty. Write them from the baby, and keep them short and sweet: 1) Thank them for the gift and name the gift, 2) State why it is the perfect gift for you, and 3) Close with how excited you are to meet them one day (or see them again).

"Signing them in the baby's name allows you to write in simple language and get away with it!"
—*Marlo Greenspan, Boyds, MD*

"I had written all my return addresses ahead of time and also set up a database, so I could record who had sent what gift. That way, I could keep track of what was given and also if I sent them a thank-you card."
—*Angel Broussard, Lake Charles, LA*

"I did the shower thank-you notes right away, before the baby came. With every other gift, I did one as they came. Enlist the help of your husband! Also, at my shower, someone had everyone write their name and address on an envelope to save me the hassle of doing that myself. That was pretty thoughtful."
—*Susan Lowry, Mooresville, IN*

"Just plan on doing five a day. If you have more time, do more. If you don't overwhelm yourself, it's so much easier, especially if your little one is already here. Keep them out and somewhere convenient. As you pass by, scrawl one out, and they will be done before you know it!"
—*Becky Messerli, Chesterfield, MI*

"I had a girlfriend with beautiful handwriting help me. I dictated everything, and she wrote them out."
—*Holly Cocchiola, Bethlehem, CT*

"Make it easy for the next mom you give a gift to by doing your thank-you note for her! When my son was born, our neighbor gave us a gift and included a preaddressed, prestamped, and prewritten thank-you and said she would be offended if we didn't use it.

"I opened the card and found a thank-you note she had written to herself (and addressed and stamped) inside. It said, 'Dear (her name), Thank you so much for the great gift.' Then it had a check off area that read, 'It was the best gift we've ever received; We really liked the gift; The gift was not really our taste and is going in the regift pile.'

"I am probably mixing up the words, but I thought it was really funny and very clever. I did end up using it. Any time-saver on the millions of thank-yous one needs to write after having a baby is so helpful."

—Susan Benovitz, Gaithersburg, MD

EDITOR'S NOTE: True confession time—I was the one who did this for Suzy. I remembered how stressful writing thank-you notes was for me, and I wanted to help her out. Now I do this for all baby gifts, as long as I know the parents receiving them have a sense of humor. I have had one mom tell me some of her relatives saw the note and thought it was rude. Obviously, they didn't understand the intent. If you make it clear that you're being funny *and* trying to help, most moms will appreciate your note even more than the gift itself.

CHAPTER SIX

TAKING CARE OF MOMMY

So is this motherhood gig what you expected? Long, lazy mornings spent nuzzling your sweet little angel, then letting him sleep contentedly, while you do a household project or catch up with old friends on the phone? Not exactly? Yeah, that stuff is only for diaper commercials or TV sitcoms where the TV mom (who doesn't even really have kids) gets a staff of twenty to do her hair and makeup every day.

The good news is motherhood *is* just about the most exhilarating and enriching experience you'll ever have. *Really.* You just have to get to the point where at three in the afternoon you can say with absolute certainty, that you did, in fact, brush your teeth today. And, honestly, it won't be long before that day comes.

In the meantime, we'll give you the skinny on taking care of yourself. We're talking just the basics here, like how to get a shower when your breasts are engorged, your phone is ringing off the hook, and you don't know whether the baby will wake up wailing for food in two minutes or twenty. Like what to say to those incredibly annoying (yet well-meaning) relatives who insist on sharing their pearls of child-rearing wisdom with you on a daily basis. Like how to cope with the stresses of new motherhood, make sure you get the maximum sleep possible, and most important of all, get daddy to pitch in and help.

Getting a Shower

You'd think this would be no big deal. After all, they are just babies. It's not like they're going to unlock your front door and go play in the street if you take a five-minute shower. But getting a shower on a regular basis was one of the most challenging tasks we faced as new moms. Here's what we discovered.

FOUR SIMPLE TIPS
FOR GETTING A SHOWER EVERY DAY

1. Put the baby in a swing or bouncy seat in the bathroom with you.
2. Do it while the baby's sleeping.
3. Do it when your husband is home or when a friend or relative can come over and watch the baby.
4. Bring the baby in the shower with you.

"My children loved the hum of the shower, so I'd take them into the bathroom with me. They would sit in a bouncy seat and look around, while mom took the fastest showers in history! When I'd get out, I'd have to hurry up and start blow-drying my hair, because they liked the hum of that, too."
—*Tracy Pritchard, Kyle, TX*

"I sure remember those days! I usually tried to get a shower when they napped or put them in the bouncy seat in the bathroom. When my son was older, I put him in the playpen with a video on. I don't think I rinsed all of the shampoo out most of the time, because I was always just trying to hurry up and get out."
—*Anna Marie Menta, Clifton Heights, PA*

"Before the baby is even born, or as soon as you think of it afterward, figure out the best time of day for your partner to watch the baby while you shower. Don't expect him to think about the fact that you need one, unless you get really stinky! Fifteen minutes in

the shower can do you so much good, both mentally and physically. For the first eighteen months of my son's life, it was my daily escape from the demands of motherhood."
—Rachel Hulan, Lake Forest, CA

"I wait until my husband gets home from work. He can spend some time with our daughter playing, bonding, reading, etc., while I get some 'me' time."
—Melissa Best, Avella, PA

Dealing with the Onslaught of Unwanted Advice

We got so much unsolicited advice as new moms that many of us felt as if we had been brandished with an invisible sign that said, "New Mom: Feel Free to Dump All Your Beliefs, Judgements, and Opinions About Child-Rearing on Me."

The worst offenders by far were well-meaning relatives. They questioned and challenged everything we did, from breastfeeding (or not) to sleeping with the baby (or not), using the pacifier (or not), taking the baby out too often (or not at all), and on and on.

In a moment, we'll share with you the best ways to cope with this advice—what, specifically, to do and say—but first we want to remind you that these are people who mean well. It's hard to put yourself in their position, but let's try to look at the situation a little differently.

Think about all the grief you're enduring now over, say, your decision to breastfeed. You know it's the right choice for you and your baby, but your mother swears you were exclusively formula-fed and turned out just fine. Moreover, she thinks breastfeeding is "yucky" and that you shouldn't do it in public.

This annoys you to no end, especially since you struggled for weeks before getting the hang of it. At first, your nipples were sore and you worried the baby wasn't gaining weight. Now, even though everybody claims breastfeeding burns a lot of calories, your body seems to be hanging on to those last ten pounds for dear life. You've had to deal with nasty comments from relatives and total strangers when you feed your baby in public, not to mention incomparable sleep deprivation and an inability to go anywhere by yourself for more than an hour and a half at a time. Still, you are delighted to be able to provide your baby with this ideal form of nourishment and the lifelong health benefits breastfeeding offers.

Now let's fast forward. Pretend that after all this, your daughter, the one you nursed for a year, is now grown up and pregnant with her own daughter. When you ask her about breastfeeding, she wrinkles her nose and says, "No way," making it clear the topic is not open for discussion. Would you keep your mouth shut? Would you just say, "Oh, I didn't realize you felt that way," and leave it at that? Probably not.

That's how your mother and mother-in-law feel now. Sure, times have changed and what worked for them may not work for you. Heck, it may even now be considered dangerous (think tummy sleeping, no car seats, and, my personal favorite, walkers). But the bottom line is: They were new moms once, too. And they struggled with sleep deprivation, sickness, colic, and many of the same things you're struggling with now. They also love you and want the best for you and your baby (their grandchild), so it's only natural that they want to share what they've learned.

It helps if you appreciate their perspective, but they still need to respect that you are the mother, and you and your husband are the only ones who get votes in how to raise your child. They can suggest, they can comment, but the decisions are yours and yours alone. Here's how we recommend setting boundaries with meddling relatives.

THE FIVE EASIEST WAYS TO
DEAL WITH UNWANTED ADVICE AND INTRUSIONS

1. Make it clear that you need to make these choices and mistakes by yourself.

2. Thank them for their advice. Then do what you want anyway without explanation.

3. Avoid discussions about your parenting choices. Change the subject when it comes up.

4. Tell them the doctor told you to do it this way.

5. Join a support group of other new moms and vent!

"Adopt a 'Don't Ask, Don't Tell' policy. Keep it social unless you're discussing this with someone whom you know will understand."
—*Brenda Brown, Kapolei, HI*

"Remember that many things that mothers and mothers-in-law say to you contain outdated advice or are a trip down memory lane for them. Boy, do the stories change after thirty years. Gee, did you know my husband walked at seven months? Each decade, he became a month more advanced. It's probably highly unlikely that he walked before nine or ten months, but there's no use ruining a good legend in his family."
—*Brenda Dintiman, M.D., Fairfax, VA*

"Say, 'I know I am a new mom, but I would like to learn what my baby likes on my own.'"
—*Alisa Norris, Plano, TX*

"A lot of times I will say something like, 'Ah, isn't that interesting. I'll have to look into that' or something equally noncommital. That way, I am not starting an argument, but I am not committing to following their advice either."
—*Heather Meininger, Charlotte, NC*

"The easiest thing to tell people is, 'The pediatrician told us that———— is fine or okay.' That one sentence helps with most

questions. Also, just smile and say something like, 'Oh, that's something to think about.'"
—*Kris Rivas, Denver, CO*

"Smile politely, but refuse to back up/defend your choices in parenting. Citing examples/studies makes family members think that your parenting method is up for discussion. Just nod and try to change the subject as soon as possible."
—*Rachel Bailey, Bay Minette, AL*

Time for You

HOW TO HANDLE IT WHEN YOU'RE SICK OF PLAYING PEEK-A-BOO, CAN'T FACE ANOTHER LOAD OF LAUNDRY, AND JUST WANT TO ESCAPE

Your first instinct as a new mom is to do everything you can to make your baby happy and comfortable. And naturally, that's important. But it's also important to take care of yourself. In fact, in our experience, the happiest, most well-taken-care-of mommies have the happiest and most well-cared-for babies. It's true! So put your needs first: It's good for you and your baby. Here's how.

FIVE SECRETS OF THE MOST RELAXED AND ENERGETIC NEW MOMS

1. Get out of the house.
2. When daddy comes home, take mommy time.
3. Do something you enjoy BY YOURSELF.
4. Schedule a regular period of time for yourself every day.
5. Connect with other moms.

"Leave the house. Twofold reason: It calms the baby down just by driving around, and other people always manage to put things

into perspective for you when they see the baby in the park or the market and say, 'What a beautiful baby!' I just love to have a conversation with an adult with whom I couldn't agree more."
—*Michelle Gebhard, D.O., White Plains, NY*

"I take little breaks whenever I can. I hire a mother's helper to hold the baby while I take a bath, or I'll go out for coffee for an hour and leave the baby with my husband. Time away, out of the house, is truly necessary from time to time."
—*Stacey Sklar, Oakland, CA*

"Attempt to plan activities for yourself while your husband watches the kids. Whether it is a trip to the library or a chance to go for a walk or a half hour to sit and read in peace, these times are SO vital to your well-being. I think it is important for every mom to have a little of this time every day. It gives you a break and allows you to be a better mom in the long run, since you will feel more refreshed after a break."
—*Jana Bell, London, OH*

"Talk to other moms. This was a lifesaver for me. It helps put things into perspective. Other moms know what you are going through and can offer advice. I would also recommend setting aside at least thirty minutes a day for yourself. This will help maintain your individuality. New moms need to remember that they are people, too."
—*Desiree Bochman, Paradise, CA*

"Ask a friend or family member to watch the baby, even just for an hour, once a week to start. Take a walk, get outside, get a haircut, do something fun. Moms also need time with their partners to be a couple—without the baby. Try for once a week to have a date. Any small amount of exercise is good, too."
—*Krystal Johnston, M.D. Manistee, MI*

"Make sure you can plan a day just for you, at least once a month. Mine was going to the salon to have my hair cut and col-

ored. It was so nice to get away and relax while being pampered. And then you look like a new person when you leave!"
—*Katie Conroy, Palos Hills, IL*

"I go to a coffee shop or have lunch at a restaurant (yes, even alone) where I don't have to unwrap my food."
—*Sara Dixon, Grimesland, NC*

"At first this will be hard to do, but I recommend trying to get up about an hour earlier than everyone else to read/exercise/sip coffee, etc. It will make your day go much more smoothly, and you won't feel so deprived by the end of the day."
–*Rachel Bailey, Bay Minette, AL*

Coping with Sleep Deprivation

Have you noticed that the very same people who tell you to sleep when the baby sleeps also advise you to pretreat spit-up stains immediately and expect you to serve them refreshments (and clean up) when they visit? They don't seem to understand (or remember) what new motherhood is like.

Before we had our babies, we thought sleeping when the baby slept would be no big deal. We imagined the schedule would go something like this:

1. Baby wakes.
2. Feed the baby.
3. Play with the baby.
4. Put baby down for a nap.
5. Take a nap, clean the house, prepare dinner, do a craft project, paint the living room, etc.

In reality, it was more like this:

1. Baby wakes.
2. Feed the baby.

3. Spend ten minutes coaxing a burp out of gassy baby.

4. Change baby's diaper.

5. Carry baby around the house, while attempting to accomplish something, like wash a glass that is so cruddy, it is starting to grow mold.

6. Baby cries.

7. Try to soothe baby with assorted tricks—swaddling, bouncing, etc. Is she hungry again?

8. Repeat steps 2 through 6.

9. Baby falls asleep—finally!

10. Mommy runs around the house like a maniac, trying to figure out what to do first with these blessed moments of freedom—after all, who knows how long they'll last?

The problem is there is so much to do and nap time is the perfect time to get it all done. At first, you can't wait until nap time to get a peaceful shower, return the twenty phone messages that were left on your answering machine, or wash last night's dinner dishes. Later, when you come down from the adrenaline high of the first days of motherhood, you feel so exhausted and overwhelmed, you don't allow yourself to sleep because there is so much to be done around the house—the laundry, the dishes, the trash, the baby announcements, etc.

There's no way around it: Motherhood is a big job. The problem is you can't do it well if you aren't rested. Luckily, there are some important tricks you can use to make sure you get your rest. The key is to make sleep your top priority. You may have noticed we've mentioned this before. THAT'S BECAUSE IT'S REALLY, REALLY IM-PORTANT. Ahem. Not trying to scream here, but we want to make sure you get the message: Baby care is number one. Sleep is number two. Get it? Good. Here's how to make that happen in the real world.

THE EIGHT EASIEST WAYS
TO MAKE SURE YOU GET YOUR SLEEP

1. Take turns with your partner getting up at night.

2. Let the house go; lower your standards for what chores need to be done, how well and how fast.

3. If you must do chores, do them for a limited time, then rest, or rest first and set an alarm to wake up and do chores.

4. Put the baby in a sling, baby carrier, playpen, or other safe place and do chores while he or she is awake, then rest while the baby is napping.

5. Have friends or relatives come over to watch the baby so you can nap, or hire a sitter so you can sleep—really!

6. Cosleep or keep the baby close by in your room at night, which can shorten nighttime interruptions.

7. Splurge on a cleaning service, baby nurse, or nanny to get you through the first few weeks or months.

8. Nap with the baby.

"Have your husband take over baby duties for a while so you can nap. Take turns getting up at night. If you are nursing, leave a bottle of breast milk for him to feed the baby."
—Amy McDonald, Buffalo, MN

"Find a way to get one solid block of sleep every twenty-four hours. Husbands are notoriously bad at getting up in the middle of the night, but mine was willing to do feedings in the late evening, when he was up anyway. So I'd go to bed at 8, and he'd do any feedings that happened before midnight, when he went to bed. If he fed the baby right at 12, I could usually sleep until about 2. Six hours of uninterrupted sleep—WOW!

"Many babies will go back to sleep for an hour or two after they first wake up/eat/play in the morning (mine did it until he was six months old). So I would always go right back to bed

when he did. Those extra two hours were a lifesaver after a short night."
—*Gail Vold Greco, Minneapolis, MN*

"When the baby was sleeping, I set an alarm for twenty minutes. I did all I could in that twenty minutes and then I rested. I did that each and every time she slept throughout the day, and by the end of the day, I had done what I needed to do. With two now, it can be a little harder, but I still do the twenty-minute thing and then have the older one rest with mom."
—*Ange Gregory, Stanwood, IA*

"Babies usually take more than one nap a day, so decide if you are going to do chores during the morning or afternoon nap. Then stick with the plan. Nap at least one time with the baby, and then you will probably be able to stay up a little later in the evening. I also paid a neighborhood girl to come to my house and watch the baby while I went up to my bedroom for a nap. I couldn't afford to do that every day, but it was well worth it on the days when I was feeling extremely overwhelmed and exhausted."
—*Lori Stussie, Lawrence, KS*

"Hire help. Either to clean, do the laundry, cook, etc., or to hold the baby while you do the work. Take advantage of all the visitors to either hold the baby while you get stuff done or to help bring you meals. Lower your standards and find ways to multitask whenever you can. Get a Baby Björn [carrier] to put the baby in and have him or her strapped to you while you do things around the house. Go to bed at 7 or 8 p.m. for a few months. Your husband and the TV can live without you while you try to get a few moments of sleep."
—*Stacey Stevens, Alamo, CA*

"Cosleep, especially if you are nursing. It makes things much easier. Rather than being woken up by a baby crying on the monitor, your baby is right there. You'll be able to respond quicker and get baby back to sleep sooner, giving you more time to sleep, too."
—*Colleen Grace Weaver, San Lorenzo, CA*

Getting Daddy to Help

The first and most important thing you must realize about new dads is that they generally want to help. In fact, helping can make a new dad feel needed, competent, and loved. Really—it's a good thing. The problem is most new dads don't automatically jump up first to change a diaper, comfort a crying baby, or wash the dishes. Truth be told, most of the time they don't even notice. That doesn't make them self-centered or wrong; it makes them *dads,* not moms. So here's how to make sure you get the help you need without nagging or complaining.

SEVEN EFFORTLESS STEPS
TO GETTING MORE HELP FROM DADDY

1. Realize and acknowledge that he is feeling stress, too.
2. Be honest about how overwhelmed and scared you are.
3. Assume that he will automatically take on the responsibility. Don't ask for permission; just act like it's his job.
4. Make specific requests, so he knows exactly what you want.
5. Let him do things in his own way. Never nag or criticize!
6. Make it a point to show your appreciation for everything he does.
7. Encourage him to have a special bonding ritual with the baby that doesn't involve you.

"From what I've learned, most men won't offer. Hand the baby to them, and tell them what a wonderful job they are doing."
—Missi Darnell, Acton, CA

"It's often difficult for new moms to let their babies go into their husband's 'inexperienced' hands. But I promise you, it is well

worth it. Dads are a lot smarter than we give them credit for, and many times will not do things for the baby if mom is there to do them first. Leave your baby for short periods of time with your husband (you can still be in the house, just don't come to their 'rescue' every time baby whimpers). You will be surprised how quickly and how much he learns about what and how to do things for your baby. Trust him, and let him know you trust him."
—Rachel Bailey, Bay Minette, AL

"I have a husband who helps, but not the way I want it done. I have tried very hard to realize that our daughter is safe and happy even if the towel is sitting on the floor instead of on the back of the door. Most men need to be asked, as I don't think they have a clue as to what to do. And asking makes them feel wanted. The baby is not the main focus of their time, and men seem to feel left out of a lot of the activities."
—Kristin Townsend, Springboro, OH

"Sometimes I had to beg and cry. He saw me as the perfect mother, able to handle everything and all-knowing. I think part of this persona was created by my inability to admit that I was scared, unsure, and more than a little overwhelmed. I had to be honest with him and show him how scared and overwhelmed I was (as well as exhausted) before he understood he needed to really step up to the plate. It was a hard first few weeks. The hardest was the night that we started fighting about who was more tired than the other. Me, because I'm taking care of the baby all day and all night or him because he's working. He did need to help more, and we finally created a compromise, though it took some time and a few arguments."
—Jennifer Weintraub, Dallas, TX

"My husband was wonderful. He helped out so much. The hardest part was not critiquing the way he was doing things. Men just do things differently, and I had to accept the fact that as long as it was getting done, it didn't matter HOW it was getting done."
—Sherry Rennie, Rialto, CA

"Let him feel part of the mom and baby world, rather than an outsider. If he's off at work, call him and let him listen to the baby. If he's at home, show him that he is as important to the baby as you are by showing him that you trust him 100 percent with the baby.

"One of the biggest complaints I hear from guys I know with new babies is that they feel their wives are overprotective of the baby, even when they are in charge. It's hard to let go, because you took care of this baby for nine months [in the womb], but I think it's beyond important to show daddy that he is needed, and make him know that you appreciate his helping."

—*Valerie Downs, Altoona, PA*

CHAPTER SEVEN

Taking Care of Baby

Wouldn't it be nice if babies came with instructions? Or at the very least, an LED screen that told you what they needed at any given time, so you really could distinguish that hungry cry from the tired cry (a trick most of us never got the hang of, by the way). In this chapter, we'll give you our best tricks for handling some of the most common baby care challenges, from colic to constipation.

Colic

Nobody knows what causes colic, and there isn't any specific cure. But here are some strategies that have helped us ease the crying periods.

TEN PROVEN TECHNIQUES FOR CALMING, SOOTHING, AND COPING WITH A COLICKY BABY

1. Rock the baby near white noise, such as the dishwasher, vacuum cleaner, dryer, or shower.
2. Swaddle the baby.
3. Apply pressure to baby's tummy.
4. If you're breastfeeding, eliminate gassy foods such as broccoli and dairy; if formula feeding, try switching formula.
5. Use Mylicon drops, fennel tea, or gripe water if the source of discomfort is gas.

6. Go for a ride in the car.

7. Put the baby in the swing or a vibrating bouncy seat.

8. Apply something warm to the baby's tummy, like a blanket that has just come out of the dryer or a warm water bottle.

9. Take a bath with your baby.

10. Take breaks, so you're better able to deal with it.

"Stay calm yourself. If you get stressed, the baby senses it. Make sure you take small breaks. Have the father help so you don't feel overwhelmed."
—Melanie Bryant-Kelsey, Edison, NJ

"It seemed to soothe Sunny when I would hold her upside down in the 'football position' and rock her gently. If I had something interesting on TV, she would focus on that, which also helped."
—Maya Beneli, Carmichael, CA

"I rocked my baby in front of the dishwasher. The humming from the dishwasher seemed to quiet her down."
—Amy Kobler, Buffalo, NY

"I had two colicky babies. I firmly believe that my babies had colic as a reaction to adjusting to the world outside. Some babies just cry. They are overwhelmed by their new environment and can't express themselves any other way. Nothing—and I mean, NOTHING—stopped the crying. All I could do was hold them, rock them, and love them. I used ear plugs to deaden the sound. When it got to be too much, I would put my baby in the crib and walk away for a few minutes to collect myself. Constant crying can be very tiring, especially when you are already sleep-deprived. It is okay to take a five-minute break."
—Tiffany Zimmer, Baltimore, MD

"The shower, the shower, the shower! When my son had colic, we discovered that the sound of a running shower stopped his crying instantly. My husband I would take turns, sitting in the

bathroom while he listened to the shower . . . ahhh, the good old days!"
—*Staci Paro, Lynn, MA*

"My best advice for colic is to get backup. Make sure you have friends or family who can give you a break now and then, or have your partner arrange to come home early some days if the late afternoon is the bad time. Rest when your baby rests, and do some nice things for yourself. Get out and get a manicure, or get coffee and read a nice book for an hour when someone else can stay with the baby."
—*Karen Wang, M.D., Wayne, PA*

"My baby cried solidly for four months. I have TONS of experience in this department. The thing that saved my life (and my son's vocal cords) was carrying him in a sling or a front carrier, such as the Baby Björn. The first time he was carried in one, he stopped crying and fell asleep. It was a lifesaver for me. I also recommend getting in a warm bath with your baby, tightly swaddling them, holding him/her with your skin against the baby's, nursing, and a lot of patience."
—*Suzanne McMillan, Greenbrier, TN*

"With my son, after at first denying and then agreeing that he was indeed, colicky, I began to look at my diet as a nursing mom in an effort to get him through this difficult time. I eliminated all dairy products and other possibly problematic foods, such as broccoli. Though that did seem to help a little, it was not a total solution. I then told my tale of woe to a neighbor who offered to loan me her swing, and that swing became my savior the very first day we used it. My son quickly fell asleep in it each afternoon during the colic period, and we had a relatively happy baby."
—*Dana Croy, Murfreesboro, TN*

"My older daughter had colic, and I would walk around with her facing outward, so that she would be slightly bent and would

hang over my arm, and the pressure on the stomach would help. Another way that really helped and was fun for me, too, was to take her into a warm bath with me. It would relax both of us, and the warm water would soothe her stomach and her soul."
—Shannon Guay, Galloway, OH

"A lot of pacing around and swaying with them in your arms helps. Try different 'white noises,' such as a clothes dryer, hair dryer, etc."
—Rebecca Harper, Gaston, SC

Burping

Burping is all about relaxing. If you can get your baby to relax, a burp will usually come easily. But once he is uncomfortable enough to cry, it becomes more difficult. Here are our best tricks for making the burps come easily.

FIVE SIMPLE WAYS TO COAX A BURP OUT OF A GASSY BABY

1. Rub or put pressure on the baby's tummy by laying her facedown on your lap.
2. Hold baby sitting up in your lap, supporting him in front with your hand, and rubbing or patting his back.
3. Bicycle baby's legs.
4. Give baby a pacifier or something else that naturally calms her.
5. Try to make baby laugh.

"Lay baby across your lap, gently rocking the legs back and forth, while patting the baby from bottom up to the head. You can also try laying the baby on his back and bending the legs up to the tummy."
—Jeannette Eshbach, Roy, UT

"Make baby laugh . . . a burp usually follows. Really!"
—Melanie Bryant-Kelsey, Edison, NJ

"My girls always burped best when I put them in a sitting-up position. Pat the baby's back for several seconds, and if it doesn't come, you recline the baby briefly and sit her back up and try again. This works with newborns, too. Just remember to hold the baby so she has head support."
—Jessica Stygles, Toledo, OH

"I do a combination of patting and rubbing in a circular motion. Also, if the burp is still a little stubborn, I stand my daughter up on my lap and get her laughing. That definitely does it."
—Melissa Best, Avella, PA

Constipation

Constipation is a common problem, but just to be sure, it's always a good idea to discuss it with your doctor. Sometimes what you perceive as constipation is just a different bowel pattern.

SIX SIMPLE CURES FOR CONSTIPATION

1. Give the baby prune juice, apple juice, or pear juice (diluted or not, as directed by your doctor). Or if baby is older, give prune baby food or mashed prunes.
2. Massage the baby's tummy.
3. Give baby a warm bath.
4. Glycerin suppositories.
5. Make sure baby is getting enough fluids. Feed the baby (breast milk or formula) frequently.
6. Put a small amount of dark karo syrup (such as 1 tsp.) in the baby's bottle.

"Apple juice is a great way to ease constipation because it works well, but isn't too harsh. I've found that pear juice gives my daughter diarrhea, but apple juice never gives her a problem. Carrots also do the trick, if you don't mind bright orange stools!"
—Kari Lomanno, Chesapeake, VA

"When she was eating mostly solids, my daughter used to strain so hard to have a bowel movement that she'd throw up! Our pediatrician recommended a daily serving of prunes, and it worked wonders. Prunes are a great way to relieve constipation."
—*Jessica Stygles, Toledo, OH*

"Remember that constipation is hard stools, not just infrequent stools. Also remember that babies can cry and fuss and make a big production out of having a poop, but if the poop comes out soft, you don't need to worry that they are constipated. Breastfed babies, especially, can stool very infrequently because they use the milk so efficiently (once a week or less), but as long as the stool is soft, you don't have a problem. Make sure that your baby is taking enough breast milk or formula.

"Babies often get constipated at the transitions from breastfeeding to formula feeding or from going from breast milk or formula to whole milk, around a year of life. Just try to back off on the new liquid and do the transition gradually if this happens, and you're able to. If the baby is over two months, you can try an ounce or two of water once or twice a day. If the baby is less than two months, call your doctor. You can also try an ounce or two of juice (prune, pear, or apple are best), diluted with an ounce or two of water once or twice a day. Call your doctor before doing this in a child under six months of age.

"For constipation, I recommend one to two ounces of prune juice or apple juice as early as two months, an exception to my otherwise hard and fast rule of no juice before six months. I'd only recommend that people try this under advice from their physician, because constipation in a newborn can be a serious medical problem, and also because most of what parents call constipation in babies is not constipation at all, just normal infrequent stool patterns."
—*Karen Wang, M.D., Wayne, PA*

"Apple juice definitely works. A warm bath also helps."
—*Maya Beneli, Carmichael, CA*

"Push fluids. Let baby nurse or drink as much as he/she will. Increasing the fluid intake helps the body balance out fluid levels. Also, cut back on some of those first foods, like bananas and rice cereal. They tend to be binding agents that encourage constipation."

—Kris Taylor, Dallas, TX

"Being a physician, I recommend to my moms to start with one teaspoon of dark karo syrup (it has to be the dark one) in the bottle, and increase the karo syrup until you achieve the desired effect (soft poopies!).

—Tracy Bragg, M.D., Jacksonville, FL

Bathing

It's not like babies really get dirty enough to require a bath every day. Still, many moms like to make baths a daily activity because it can be calming and enjoyable for the baby. Here are our best tricks for making bath time easy and fun.

SIX STEPS TO MAKING BATH TIME EASY FOR YOU AND FUN FOR BABY

1. Gather everything you need in advance, including the phone if you absolutely can't let it ring.
2. Buy whatever tools you need to make it easy for you: a baby bathtub, mesh baby sling, bath visor for keeping soap out of his eyes when you wash his hair, etc.
3. Talk, sing, make funny faces, or use toys to make it fun.
4. Make sure the baby stays warm throughout the bath, by either adding new warm water or putting a warm washcloth on baby.
5. Take a bath with baby.
6. Make it fast.

"Gather everything in a basket, so prep time is quick. Use an infant tub. My daughter loved baths from day one. I usually sing to her and keep the water comfortably warm and keep wetting her, so she doesn't get cold. I've always used an infant tub in our bathtub, because we have a corner sink in our kitchen with a light and outlets close by, so we were afraid to use the sink. I think the bathroom stays warmer, too, since you can close the door.

"We use the Johnson's Bedtime Bath with Lavender and Chamomile and the Johnson's Soothing Vapor Bath when she has a cold."
—*Anna Marie Menta, Clifton Heights, PA*

"Invest in a newborn tub with a sling. Wet babies are slippery. Make sure the water is nice and warm, but not hot, and sing his or her favorite song. Warm the towel in the dryer to ease the transition from the tub."
—*Angela Anderson, Seattle, WA*

"Keep the room as warm as possible and don't worry about getting water everywhere!"
—*Crystal Burriss, Raleigh, NC*

"Bath time at first was terrible for us. I heated her towels and lowered the light in the room, shut the door while the water was running to make the air warm . . . I tried everything. She still screamed. I finally began to use a baby powder-scented candle in the room, and the scent seemed to do the trick with the combo of it all. I don't know what it was, but it was smooth sailing from there."
—*Kristin Townsend, Springboro, OH*

"Keep the baby's chest covered with a warm, wet towel that you dunked into the bathwater. Make sure you keep the towel warm by redunking into the bathwater during the bath. Also, have some water running close by. The sound of water can be soothing. Singing also helps."
—*Suzanne McMillan, Greenbrier, TN*

Sleep

Sleep takes on a whole new meaning once you become a mom. Before you had kids, you might have craved things like a new car, nice clothes, a beautiful home, or a nice vacation. Now you'd trade it all for a good night's sleep. The key, of course, is getting baby to sleep through the night. Here are our best tricks.

EIGHT SURE-FIRE STRATEGIES FOR GETTING BABY TO SLEEP THROUGH THE NIGHT

1. Have a nighttime routine.
2. Try to teach baby to put herself to sleep at an early age, by putting her down while still awake.
3. Make sure baby has a full belly, a clean diaper, and is tired.
4. Play soft music or white noise at bedtime.
5. Let baby cry it out for a time, as long as he is at least six weeks old and has proven he is able to sleep through the night (i.e., he has slept for five to six hours at a stretch without needing a feeding).
6. Sleep with your baby.
7. When baby wakes at night, keep it dark and quiet, so she can get back to sleep quickly.
8. Give baby a comfort object (like a stuffed animal or other favorite lovey) or a blanket.

"Setting up a bedtime routine worked best for us (and still works best for us now that our children are older). Dinner, playtime, bath, and bed, or any routine, for that matter, helps the child get into the mind-set that it's time to go to bed. If the child is still nursing or taking a bottle, feeding him or her before bed always helps, too."
—*Shannon Guay, Galloway, OH*

"Give a 'sleepy-time' feeding right when YOU go to bed. After six months, I allowed them to cry it out for a few minutes at a time."
—*Lisa Brooks, Butler, PA*

"Try to keep a daily routine with naps and bedtime. My baby learned it was wake, eat, sleep, and repeat, with a bath before bed as well. I was able to set her down and she would go to sleep on her own most times."
—Tamara Prince, Oshawa, Ontario, Canada

"At six weeks, we started putting her to sleep in her crib. I used to give her a bottle first, but then it got to be harder and harder. Finally, we just decided to put her down awake and walk away. After three nights, she was sleeping through the night with no problems. I never read the Ferber book [*Solve Your Child's Sleep Problems* by Richard Ferber], but it is the Ferber method. To make it easier, I recruited some mom friends who were willing to try it at the same time. We would call each other to talk, and that made it easy for the crying nights in the beginning."
—Susan Dobratz, Plymouth, MA

"I make sure that if my children wake up during the night, I never talk to them. I might do something so they know I am there (like patting their backs), but if I talk to them, they will start to wake up. I always provide the same comfort object, usually a familiar blankie."
—April McConnell, Birdsboro, PA

"We found the best way for everyone to get the most sleep was to keep our son in bed with us. In order to make sure that we were cosleeping in a safe manner, we consulted several books, including some by Dr. Bill Sears and Dr. Jay Gordon, which had wonderful information. The funny thing is that we were adamantly opposed to the idea of cosleeping before our son was born, but now that we are parents, we have found that it can really benefit both child and parents."
—Rachel Hulan, Lake Forest, CA

Coping with an Early Wake-Up Time

When your baby is two months old and sleeps through the night, but wakes up at 5 a.m., you're just happy he slept through the night; you don't care about the early wake-up time. But a 5 a.m. wake-up time gets really old after a few months, especially if you're not naturally an early riser yourself. Here are the best ways to cope.

THE SIX SMARTEST WAYS
TO DEAL WITH EARLY RISERS

1. Let the baby cry a little bit (or a lot) and see if she goes back to sleep.
2. Top baby off with a later night feeding, say around 11 p.m. or midnight.
3. Feed baby, but don't turn on the lights, and put him right back to sleep.
4. Put baby to sleep earlier in the evening.
5. Put toys in the crib and let baby play alone for a while.
6. Adjust your own schedule to accommodate the early wake-up time (e.g., go to bed earlier and take naps).

"Try feeding the baby without turning on any lights or making any noise. I found that my daughter would still think it was time to sleep if it was a quiet, dark atmosphere, whereas if I turned lights on, she was up for the day."
—Billie Smith, Turpin, OK

"When your baby is old enough to sit up on her own, put a few toys, books, etc., in her crib to keep her amused. Bring her into bed with you and put on one of the Baby Einstein videos and let her watch that while you try to get a few extra minutes of sleep. If she's definitely up and wants to be entertained, decide that maybe exercise isn't such a bad idea after all, and put her in a stroller or the Baby Björn and go for a walk. At least, it will help you wake up a bit. Then take a nap later when she does."
—Stacey Stevens, Alamo, CA

"My first would wake up at the crack of dawn and need attention and entertainment. She was not even content to lie in bed and nurse. Lying in bed trying to get her to sleep made me feel even

worse. I learned to cope by just resigning myself to starting the day at that hour. I would get up, shower with her (which she liked), have my coffee, and then go somewhere that opened really early, like the grocery store, a coffee shop, or farmers' market. She was happy to go out, and I felt like I was not the only human awake. (Also, the shower and coffee really took the edge off the morning.) On weekends, my husband would get up with her, so I could sleep in once in a while. Also, I had to discipline myself to go to bed at 8:30 or whenever she was down for the night, despite the temptation to have that free time to myself."
—*Diana Molavi, M.D., Baltimore, MD*

"I treated the 5 a.m. feeding as a night feeding. I would change the twins and feed them, but not talk to them, and I kept the lights very low. That way, they were not stimulated into an awake state and went right back to sleep for two more hours!"
—*Lori Vance, Henderson, NV*

"It may seem silly, but I would suggest an earlier bedtime. I think some people tend to put their kids down too late in hopes that they will sleep later, but that often doesn't work. Also, assuming the baby isn't still waking at night to eat, I wouldn't jump at his first little cry or movement. Wait a minute or two to make sure he really is awake prior to going and checking on him."
—*Jana Bell, London, OH*

Seven Foolproof Tricks for Getting Baby to Nap

1. Watch for clues that baby is getting sleepy and put him down as soon as you see the first sign (e.g., rubbing eyes, yawning, etc.).
2. Get baby in the habit of napping at home in the crib (or wherever she usually naps), and make sure you're home at nap time.
3. Establish a nap routine, based on baby's typical napping pattern.

4. Do stimulating activities before nap time, so baby is tired.

5. Give baby time to fall asleep (i.e., let him cry a bit) after you put him down.

6. Take a nap with baby.

7. If all else fails, take baby for a ride in the car.

"I have found that it helps to watch for clues that the baby is getting sleepy (rubbing eyes, etc.). Set up a nap time routine, kind of like a bedtime routine, but shorter, and follow it every day. If baby is extra fussy, walks outside or car rides work great!"
—*Ange Gregory, Stanwood, IA*

"I used the cry-it-out method at six months. It was a hard week, but now he's a great sleeper, and we're still sticking to a regular nap schedule. We do not go to things if they are during nap time. I also never put any toys or other distractions in the crib. It's important that babies are put in awake. They will be better sleepers as they get older."
—*Carolyn Dunn, Morristown, NJ*

"Routine, routine, routine! No matter what you have going on, if you are having trouble getting the baby to nap, set a routine and stick to it. Babies thrive on routine and so will you! For example, just after lunch, change her diaper, read a story, rock her for ten minutes and put her in her bed. After a few days, she should get used to your routine. Having the baby know what to expect is half the battle."
—*Stephanie Smith, Alexandria, KY*

"Make sure the baby gets some active play or fresh air or both. A walk in the stroller outside always does the trick for us, and it gives mom some easy exercise. Make sure baby has a fresh diaper, is fed and has had plenty to drink, so that any of those needs don't interfere with the need for sleep."
—*Suzanne McMillan, Greenbrier, TN*

"I suggest lying down with your baby and nursing to sleep. Also, watch your baby's tired signs and don't let her get overtired or she won't be able to go to sleep without a real struggle. *Secrets of the Baby Whisperer* [Tracy Hogg, Melinda Blau, Ballantine] suggests starting the nap time routine by the second yawn, and I've found that this helps."

—Jennifer Weintraub, Dallas, TX

CHAPTER EIGHT

FOOD AND NUTRITION

We moms spend untold hours agonizing over what, how much, and how often our babies eat. At first, we worry if they're getting enough to eat, then we worry if the broccoli we've eaten has given our breastfed babies gas or if the formula we've used is upsetting their tummies.

When our babies graduate to solids, we wonder whether our babies will ever eat anything from a spoon without spitting it out, which order we should introduce new fruits and vegetables, and if organic baby food is worth the extra cost.

And before we know it, that baby is a toddler, chowing down on spaghetti and fish sticks on a daily basis, and we're trying to figure out how to get her to eat more vegetables or at least consume something besides yogurt and macaroni and cheese.

This chapter covers all those feeding issues and more. From how to cope with nursing soreness to which type of formula is best, from our favorite brand of baby food to getting picky eaters to eat vegetables, it's all here. So let's dig in!

Breastfeeding

There is no question about it: Breastfeeding is the healthiest form of nutrition for your baby. And if done long enough, it can have wonderful health benefits for you, too. But it isn't always the simplest skill in the world to master. Some babies latch on easily and comfortably from the beginning. Others—and their mommies—need some instruction to get the hang of it. Below are our favorite ways to prepare for breast-feeding and our top remedies for relieving any discomfort you might feel.

HOW TO PREPARE FOR BREASTFEEDING

1. Take a breastfeeding class.
2. Read books about breastfeeding.
3. Talk to friends who've breastfed.
4. Get support from your partner in advance.

"I had no idea breastfeeding would be difficult. I'd say talk to your closest girlfriends for the whole truth. And many hospitals offer breastfeeding classes as part of their birth prep classes."
—*Carolyn Dunn, Morristown, NJ*

"If you have inverted or flat nipples, wear the nipple shields for at least two weeks before delivery. It makes things so much easier."
—*Tara Betteridge, Fort Lewis, WA*

"The best way a mom can prepare (emotionally and physically) for nursing is to surround herself with people who will help and support her in her decision to breastfeed. Before our child was born, we consulted with our doula [birth attendant] about breastfeeding. Also, we attended a breastfeeding class offered at the hospital and joined an online group that focused on breastfeeding."
—*Monique Rivera-Rogers, Champaign, IL*

"I can't emphasize enough how important it is to take a breast-feeding class. Contrary to popular opinion, breastfeeding does not always come naturally. It's definitely something that needs to be learned, and you're certainly better off knowing what you should do than trying to figure it out after delivery. The $25 that I

spent on the breastfeeding class was probably the most worth-while $25 I spent during the entire pregnancy."
—*Eliza Chin, M.D., Piedmont, CA*

THE TEN MOST EFFECTIVE REMEDIES FOR NURSING DISCOMFORT

1. Use lanolin, especially the Lansinoh and PureLan brands, on your nipples.
2. Rub some expressed milk on your nipples, and let them air-dry.
3. Contact a lactation consultant or La Leche League (800-LA-LECHE; www.lalecheleague.org) for help.
4. Replace nursing pads frequently.
5. Expose your breasts to natural sunlight for a few minutes per day.
6. Avoid putting soap on your breasts.
7. Put warm compresses on your breasts.
8. Use Gerber's Breast Therapy gel pads, hot/cold packs, and balm.
9. Wear breast shields.
10. Nurse frequently, and try to relax.

"I used a cream made by Lansinoh. I started putting it on about a week before I delivered and kept putting it on after she was born. It didn't prevent soreness 100 percent, but it sure did help! It is also safe for the baby and doesn't need to be washed off."
—*Debby Madrid, Elkhart, IN*

"Work with a lactation consultant. Many hospitals have one available to work with you when you're still in the hospital, and some insurance plans will cover visits in the weeks following. The one-on-one advice is really valuable.

"Don't be afraid to supplement. If you simply aren't making enough milk, you need to provide nutrition. If you just can't make nursing work, don't beat yourself up. The guilt can be over-whelming when you're in the middle of the process, but if formula

works better for you and your baby, it can sometimes be the best decision. A happy, well-fed baby is the goal. Breast may be best, but formula is just fine, too."
—*Gail Vold Greco, Minneapolis, MN*

"Express some of the breast milk after each feeding and let it dry on the breast. The protein from the milk itself supposedly helps the skin to heal. Keep the nipples dry and exposed to air. When my nipples were the most sore, I literally closed all the curtains and paraded around the house bare-chested—much to the horror of my mother. But you have to do what you have to do. You should also make sure that there isn't something wrong with your positioning that is causing the sore nipples. The entire nipple should be in your baby's mouth, so that it is not pulled back and forth. Use pillows to prop up your baby so that he/she doesn't slip back."
—*Eliza Chin, M.D., Piedmont, CA*

"Avoid using soap on the nipples when showering. If your nursing pads get even slightly moist, replace them immediately."
—*Claire Bienvenu, Slidell, LA*

"For me, taking hot showers or just wetting and draping washcloths over my nipples alleviated my nipple soreness the most. I had to continually reheat the washcloths with water for it to be effective."
—*Christina Stevens, Endicott, NY*

"Patience and commitment are two of the best friends a nursing mother can have. In addition, surround yourself with other moms who nurse and any other support system (especially from dad) that you can find. Physically speaking, the most important aspect of nursing is to eat well and often and to continue your water intake at around 64 ounces per day, at least while your milk supply is coming in and getting regular. Don't give up! Your milk is always with you, and it is the best thing you can give your baby."
—*Dana Croy, Murfreesboro, TN*

"Nurse as often as baby would like and in a place where you can relax. Educate yourself as to ways and aids (herbs, etc.) that can increase your milk supply. Surround yourself with people who can help you and support you from the beginning until you and baby mutually decide to wean."
—*Monique Rivera-Rogers, Champaign, IL*

"Believe it or not, the best relief for sore nipples was some natural sunlight. Sure, it sounds a little risqué, but even a little sunlight on the porch for ten minutes a day helped the cracked nipples that resulted from my first baby not putting the whole nipple in her mouth. The La Leche League is a wealth of information and will help you and the baby become great with nursing.

"Don't give up just because you need to go back to work. Many babies will still nurse morning and evening and midnight even if you feed them bottles of formula during the day. They love the bonding when you come home. Don't forget to go to your dermatologist if you develop cracking and possibly a yeast infection. They know lots of secrets about healing the skin."
—*Brenda Dintiman, M.D., Fairfax, VA*

"I used the cotton nursing pads, and when I put a clean pair on, it felt like heaven. Get lots of whatever breast pads you choose, so you can put clean ones on whenever you need to."
—*Shelly Knight, Longmont, CO*

"Take a disposable diaper soaked in hot water, then apply it to the breast for engorgement. For sore nipples, try the special bandages to be applied on burns. This cools the nipples and helps them heal when they are raw and bleeding."
—*Denine Scallen, Sammamish, WA*

"Gerber has a Breast Therapy line with cooling gel pads, reusable hot/cold packs, and balm. It's an excellent line that I would definitely recommend."
—*Angel Smith, Brooksville, FL*

"Contact a lactation consultant at your hospital or NICU. If they are not available, contact your local chapter of the La Leche League to have a consultant come to you. These women are invaluable!

"You may never get the hang of it. That's OK. My boys were too tiny at birth to nurse, and by the time they were strong enough, neither one could figure it out well enough to get what they needed from the breast. Since I had been pumping successfully from their birth, I simply continued to do so, giving them expressed milk in bottles. They had 100 percent breast milk the first thirteen months of their lives through bottles alone and did just great! I certainly didn't miss out on any bonding with all the hugging and snuggling we did during feedings, and the best part was that my husband got to play an active role as well."
—*Jenna Haldeman, Portland, OR*

"Relaxation is the key to breastfeeding. A recliner worked well for us. You can create your own little spot with the TV remote control or radio and water. My husband was fantastic about making the nursing area comfortable, and it helped make him feel a part of feeding time."
—*Wendy Douglas, Margate, FL*

THE FIVE NURSING ACCESSORIES
WE CAN'T LIVE WITHOUT

1. Boppy or other nursing pillow
2. Nursing pads
3. Nursing bra
4. Lansinoh
5. A good electric breast pump—we recommend the Medela Pump In Style

"The Medela breast pump is an absolute must! For many products in this world, there are several quality brands to choose from and little difference between them. With breast pumps, however, it has been my observation that everyone loves Medela and struggles with all the other ones. I bought a car cigarette-lighter

adapter for mine, and I was able to pump on the road. My pump enabled me to breastfeed for two years with little inconvenience."
—Sarah Pletcher, East Lansing, MI

"A Boppy pillow is a definite 'must have.' It makes positioning the baby much easier and helps with latching on. I use my Boppy all the time and my baby is almost three months old. I've even mastered reading the newspaper while the baby nurses propped on the Boppy."
—Jonalee Fernatt, Ulrichsville, OH

"My favorite nursing accessory is my breast pump. I use the Medela Pump In Style, which is stylish, lightweight, and easy to take anywhere. I use it not only to express milk while at work, but also to increase my milk supply quickly when the baby grows (I just pump in between feedings for a couple of days)."
—Rivka Stein, M.D., Brooklyn, NY

"You need a good quality nursing bra, some nursing pads (disposable or washable), a Boppy pillow, Lansinoh, and a water bottle to keep mom hydrated."
—Megan Miles, Marysville, WA

"The Boppy pillow was a must! I also loved my reclining rocker in the family room. Big, comfy shirts are a must and blankets to cover you when company is over."
—Daryl D'Angelo, Sewell, NJ

"I bought the top-of-the-line Medela Pump In Style. I love it. It has helped me through sore nipples, engorgement, etc. It also guarantees that I can get out of the house. There is no reason to buy a new Pump In Style, however. Medela strongly discourages buying and selling used pumps and says it is unsanitary to use a pump someone else has used. Baloney! It is very easy to buy new breast cups, tubes, and bottles, and the milk never gets near the motor—EVER! You should feel comfortable buying a used one from a friend or off of eBay."
—Tara Tucker, Mountain View, CA

Bottlefeeding

Bottlefeeding has gotten a bad rap in recent years. But the truth is how you feed your baby is a heck of a lot less important than how you love, care for, and raise your baby. Let's face it: Giving your baby a bottle isn't going to be the primary factor influencing his lifelong health. It isn't going to determine the closeness of your relationship with your baby, and it certainly isn't going to be the defining factor in whether or not she goes to Harvard.

So if you choose to bottlefeed (or it just works out that way), relax. No one's going to report you to the nipple police. And even if you choose to breastfeed, you still may need bottles for those times you're out or you want someone else to take a feeding.

The key in choosing the correct bottle is to try a few on your baby before you commit to one style. Some babies seem to do better with one type of bottle. Other babies have a preference for a certain type of nipple. And still others have issues, such as gassiness or reflux, for which certain bottles are better suited.

OUR TWO FAVORITE BOTTLES

1. Avent
2. Playtex nursers

"I like the Playtex disposable bottles. There's no washing bottles. You just need to wash the nipples. That's it."
—*Aamina Masood, Richardson, TX*

"I like the Playtex nursers with silicone nipples. It makes going back and forth between the breast and bottle easier, and it's nice to be able to toss out the liners. Drop-in liners are a must for these. The others don't hold as much and are a pain to drape over the sides."
—*Becky Messerli, Chesterfield, MI*

TO CONTRIBUTE TO THE NEXT EDITION,
VISIT WWW.GALLAGHERGUIDE.COM

"The Avent bottles are wider, which made them easier to clean. They also have handle attachments, which made it much easier when my baby started holding her own bottle."
—*Michelle Laney, Helena, AL*

"I found my son likes the Playtex nursers with disposable liners and the clear, silicone nipple the best. I feel that is the closest to the breast because: 1) the disposable, collapsible liners prevent baby from swallowing too much air, and 2) the clear silicone nipples allow the baby to achieve a latch-on similar to breastfeeding, in which the bottom lip is turned outward."
—*Jonalee Fernatt, Ulrichsville, OH*

Formula

It's always a good idea to consult your baby's doctor for help in deciding which formula to use, but we'll share with you the type we recommend and why.

OUR FAVORITE TYPE

Powder

"Powder formula is by far the best. I never waste formula because I make it as I go. I prefill all my bottles with the correct amount of water. I use room-temperature water (this was recommended by the pediatrician) and then I premeasure the formula in a container I purchased in the feeding aisle of Babies R Us. No matter where I am, all I have to do is open the bottle, pour in the powder, cover, and shake. No heating and no wasted formula that has to be used up within a certain time frame."
—*Susan Dobratz, Plymouth, MA*

"You get more feedings in one can with powder, which is important for those who need the best value on a budget. It is much better to travel with. There are a variety of containers that you can carry the powder in. Some have dividers that you can put enough in each compartment for a single feeding. Also, most manufacturers make

'to-go' packets. Those are also very convenient for travel. The concentrate and ready-to-feed formulas require refrigeration once they are open; powder does not. It can go anywhere."
—*Melissa Best, Avella, PA*

"It's very easy to carry a premeasured amount and bottled water and make the formula as needed. There is no need for insulated bags/cold packs or warming formula or wondering if it's still good after you've been away a bit longer than planned. And you can always carry a 'snack-sized' premeasured amount, too."
—*Sara Dixon, Grimesland, NC*

Baby's First Cup

We recommend starting your baby on a sippy cup as early as possible—five or six months is a good time. She may not be able to do much with it at first, but it will help her get used to it, and this will make an easier transition from the bottle or breast.

OUR TWO FAVORITE BRANDS

1. Playtex
2. Avent

"My favorite cup for a baby that's just learning how to drink is the Playtex sippy cup. I look for two features in a cup: Can my baby suck the drink out with ease, and is it REALLY leakproof? I've tried many other brands that claim to be leakproof, and I keep coming back to Playtex. Your carpet and furniture will thank you!

"Plus, the Playtex cups have a convenient removable valve that makes cleaning them easy, they come in a variety of sizes, and their new insulated cup is great for keeping perishable drinks (like milk) cold and fresh."
—*Stephanie Martin, Macomb, MI*

"I am a true believer in the Avent line. My first son used only Avent bottles and then started on the Avent sippy cups at four

months! They have a beginner sippy lid that fits on the Avent bottles and handles that screw on. Then your child progresses to the older sippy line. My two-year-old still uses these at times."
—Anna Maria Johnson, Shreveport, LA

Baby Food

Breast milk or formula is your baby's most important source of nutrition during the first year, but sometime between four and six months (most pediatricians recommend six months), you'll introduce your baby to solid food.

If you want to save money on baby food, and/or you really want to know exactly what is in it, consider making your own. You can simply mash soft foods with a fork or use a food processor or blender to puree soft fruits and vegetables and store them in ice cube trays. Just thaw, warm a little, and serve.

OUR TWO FAVORITE BRANDS OF BABY FOOD

1. Gerber
2. Organic, such as Gerber Tender Harvest or Earth's Best

"I like Gerber because it's a name I trust and the smell/texture of the food is far more appealing than Beech-Nut or other brands. The Tender Harvest line had a great selection that my daughter loved. These had a smell and texture that was even better than regular Gerber."
—Marlo Greenspan, Boyds, MD

"I like Earth's Best by the Hains Celestial Group. It is 100 percent organic made with no GMOs (genetically modified organisms). What better way to start solids than with the healthiest ingredients? Only the best for our miracles."
—Monique Rivera-Rogers, Champaign, IL

"I like Gerber's organic brand [Tender Harvest]. I just want the best for Isabella, and since I don't make her food, I can at least buy her organic."
—*Kris Rivas, Denver, CO*

"I liked Earth's Best. They had the best flavors and actually looked like you might want to eat them. I especially recommend the foods that contain spinach."
—*Stacey Stevens, Alamo, CA*

Finger Foods

The most important thing we look for in first finger foods is safety. We don't want any potential choking hazards, which means foods like nuts, raisins, grapes, and hot dogs are off limits for babies until age three.

We want our babies to get off to a healthy start, so we look for foods that are not only easy to gum, but are good for them, too. And we gravitate toward foods that are easy to make, easy to take with us when we go out, and easy to clean up.

OUR NUMBER ONE FAVORITE FIRST FINGER FOOD

Cheerios

"Cheerios are the best first finger food to establish a healthy eating habit. They taste good, melt in milk readily, and are easy to store, carry, and serve. My daughter used to stick her little fingers through the holes of moistened Cheerios and make fingertip rings. She would then eat them off her fingers with relish."
—*Susan Lonergan, Woodside, CA*

"They're easy to keep in your purse. Plus, they have nutritional value, dissolve easily in a little one's mouth, and have a nice shape that works fine motor skills."
—*Karen Haas, Laurel, MD*

"There isn't a lot of sugar in them, and they are the right size for small fingers. They also get really soggy quickly, so there is not much of a choking hazard."
—Denine Scallen, Sammamish, WA

"They melt quickly in baby's mouth, they are low in sugar, and I never mind when Madyson wants to feed them to me as well."
—Lisa Bittar, Brooklyn, NY

"Cheerios can be broken in half and don't pose a severe choking hazard. They are low fat and full of good stuff for babies. They are a low-maintenance snack. You can take them anywhere with you, and they don't make a mess on the floor, in the car, or on baby's hands, mouth, or clothes."
—Shelly Huggins, Bel Air, MD

Healthy Snacks

We know that snacks are important to kids' diets, so we want them to be as satisfying and nutritious as possible. Here are our favorites.

THE FIVE SNACKS WE FEEL BEST ABOUT GIVING OUR KIDS

1. Fruit
2. Vegetables, with or without dip
3. Yogurt
4. Peanut butter and . . . apple slices, bananas, celery, etc.
5. Cheese

"Bananas with anything—peanut butter or in a smoothie. Kids love smoothies because they taste like milk shakes. They think they're getting a huge treat."
—Mari Kistler, St. Petersburg, FL

"I like Go-Gurt (yogurt in a tube). It's easy, filling, provides calcium, and is nutritious. It's also great for babies and eliminates the need for utensils."
—*Eliza Chin, M.D., Piedmont, CA*

"String cheese is not messy, and it's convenient. One stick is usually a good portion for a child. Yogurt is another favorite, as are raw carrots and dip, sliced fruit, such as grapes and watermelon, or sliced turkey."
—*Diane Bedrosian, M.D., Carlsbad, CA*

"Fruit, fruit, and more fruit! It has excellent vitamins and fiber, plus natural sugars for an extra energy boost. My son helps pick out fresh fruit at the grocery store. We have a deal that he will try some of every type of fruit he chooses and he usually enjoys them all."
—*Sylvia Anderson, Rapid City, SD*

"Kids love a cup of frozen peas! On a warm day, they are refreshing and a lot healthier than ice cream."
—*Cara Vincens, Thionville, France*

"We blanch carrot sticks to make them easier to chew. Blanching softens them and brings out more natural sweetness. Then we chill them for a little crispness and also to make them friendly to tender gums. We also go through a lot of sliced cheese."
—*Debbie Palmer, Hickory, NC*

Vegetables

Lots of kids, especially babies and toddlers like vegetables—probably because they haven't been exposed to a lot of sugary, processed foods yet. But many don't like vegetables at all, especially those with older siblings who turn their noses up at veggies. This can become a bigger problem as toddlers get older and enter the "picky eater" stage. Here are our best recommendations for coping with vegetable-averse kids.

SEVEN SMART WAYS TO GET KIDS TO EAT VEGGIES

1. Serve them with dip.
2. Cover them with cheese.
3. Hide them in pasta sauces and other foods they like.
4. Invite kids to help cook, prepare, and even grow them in your own garden.
5. Eat them yourself and offer them over and over again, without judging the response.
6. Call them by fun names, like trees for broccoli.
7. Serve them first before the rest of the meal.

"The best way to get a child to eat vegetables that they don't like is to offer some kind of sauce or dip with it. For example, my children do not like celery, but when they can dip it in peanut butter, they are more likely to eat it. The same thing goes for carrot sticks and ranch dressing or cauliflower with cheese sauce."
—*Tracy Pritchard, Kyle, TX*

"When they were very little, they loved them. Now I have one who will happily chow on veggies if there is dip/ketchup anywhere in sight. The other could find carrot in carrot cake."
—*Janette Gilman, Potomac, MD*

"I make a pasta sauce and puree vegetables and put them in the sauce."
—*Ann Stowe, Burlingame, CA*

"I was disheartened one day when Becca wouldn't eat her steamed broccoli. I mentioned that it is too bad she didn't like the 'little trees' and was preparing to take them away. When she heard me call them little trees, she changed heart, ate them, and liked them!"
—*Jennifer Rose, Ashland, MA*

"Offer veggies raw or slightly steamed (no seasoning) and a variety of dips—even ketchup can make the pickiest of eaters love broccoli."
—*Lynn Parks, Durham, NC*

"I get out the blender and make all kinds of vegetable bisques. Just add milk and cheese, and they never know what they're eating! Here's a great recipe that can be used with any number of cooked vegetables. I usually just chop the vegetables I'm using and steam them in a little metal vegetable steamer in a pot of boiling water. This recipe is my favorite for tomato bisque, but you can substitute carrots, turnips, squash, pretty much anything, for the tomatoes."

—*Rachel Bailey, Bay Minette, AL*

VEGGIE BISQUE

1 cup peeled, seeded, and chopped fresh tomatoes, or 1 14-oz. can of whole peeled tomatoes, drained

1/2 cup coarsely chopped onion

1/2 teaspoon chopped garlic

2 tablespoon olive oil

4 medium potatoes, peeled and sliced

4 cups water or chicken broth

1/2 teaspoon salt

2 teaspoon dried basil

Sour cream for garnish (or grated cheese)

Saute tomatoes, onion, and garlic in the olive oil in a large saucepan until tomato liquid is reduced and onion is soft. Add potatoes, water, and salt and bring to a boil. Reduce heat and simmer until potatoes are very tender (about thirty minutes). Add basil or your spice of choice. Turn off heat. Pour into an electric blender. Blend on low speed until the texture is to your taste. Serve hot, garnished with sour cream or cheese.

NOTE: If substituting any of the orange vegetables for the tomatoes, I substitute dill for basil and sometimes add some milk and/or cheese to the mixture after I turn off the heat to make it creamier. The possibilities for this recipe are endless, and you can disguise any vegetable that you want your kids to eat! Even broccoli! You can also whisk in wheat germ, flaxseed, anything nutritious you can think of and your kids will never know!

"I simply offer different vegetables at each meal and let my children decide what they want to try and eat. If they don't want to try it one night, no problem. I just keep offering it until they do."
—Stephanie Martin, Macomb, MI

"I got my oldest to think that carrots were candy when she was two. She liked candy corn, which are orange and yellow and shaped like carrots. One day, she was fussing about cooked carrots, as two-year-olds will do, and I just told her they were candy. She tried it and liked the natural sweetness."
—Jeannette Eshbach, Roy, UT

"My son used to eat anything under the sun until he became really good at feeding himself. Then he would only pick up certain foods and would not eat anything you tried to feed him. So now I try to hide vegetables in all sorts of things—chopped carrots and red peppers in a cheese quesadilla, sauteed zucchini or yellow squash mixed with the tomato sauce on pizza English muffins, etc. I also make a 'pizza face' with different veggies on top of the cheese, then bake them. The best idea I use I read as a tip somewhere and never forgot it. I take broccoli florets and cut off the very tip. That leaves you with a pile of green 'sprinkles.' Pour them into a grated cheese shaker (with the large holes on top) and let your child sprinkle them all over his/her food. My son loves anything with real candy sprinkles and this way, he thinks he's getting just that. Shhhh! Please don't tell him!"
—Kristi Swartz, Gaithersburg, MD

"I found that when my girls were old enough to 'help' in the kitchen, they were more than happy to eat what they helped cook, and this is another way to spend some quality time with them."
—Bobbi Annal, Spokane, WA

"I offer a variety of veggies for snacks and at meals. Try fresh, cooked, and frozen. My kids love mixed frozen veggies in a little snack cup right from the freezer. My kids also snack on fresh veg-

gies while 'helping' me prepare a salad for dinner. Finally, plant a garden. Kids love to tend the garden and snack on fresh fruits and veggies that they helped to grow."
—*Sidney Marks, Menlo Park, CA*

"Don't treat veggies any different than other foods. If you don't make a huge fuss every time your child eats something good for them, they won't know they aren't supposed to like good stuff."
—*Lori Stussie, Lawrence, KS*

"My best discovery is the PuPu platter—a large platter with seven sections. I put a different cut-up fruit and vegetable in each section and put it on the table when the kids are watching TV before dinner. The snack disappears in minutes, and the kids love it without realizing they're eating something healthy. Then, because they've had their fruits and veggies, I don't need to stress out about trying to get them to eat veggies at dinner. And it takes care of the predinner irritability."
—*Donnica L. Moore, M.D., Branchburg, NJ*

Dealing with a Picky Eater

Around eighteen months, toddlers suddenly realize that they are separate human beings, and they love to flex their independence muscles at every opportunity. A favorite way is refusing to eat—or at least refusing to eat what you serve. Some kids go through a limited diet stage, where they only eat three or four different foods, or perhaps only foods of a certain color (which, unfortunately, is never green!). Other kids just pick at what's on their plates or refuse to eat hardly anything at all. Never fear: We're here to help. These are our tried and true techniques for coping with picky eaters.

SEVEN MAGIC WAYS TO GET PICKY EATERS TO EAT

1. Stop forcing the issue. Make good choices available; then let go of whether or not he eats them.

2. Have a must-try rule: She must at least try the food before rejecting it.

3. Serve a variety of foods, and serve them over and over again (without pressure to eat them), until your child gets used to seeing them.

4. Serve creatively—cut food into fun shapes, use food coloring, serve with dip, ketchup, barbecue sauce, etc.

5. Let your child help you choose foods at the store and prepare them with you at home.

6. Reverse her meals: Serve dinner foods like chicken nuggets for breakfast and cereal for dinner.

7. Don't cook separate meals for them.

"Mix up your meals a little. There's nothing wrong with having spaghetti for breakfast and waffles for dinner if that's what your toddler wants. And be patient. Most toddlers need a new food presented ten to fifteen times before they will eat it. Keep trying and eventually the food will start to disappear off the tray."
—*Jenna Haldeman, Portland, OR*

"We have a one-bite rule. You don't have to eat anything you don't like, but you do have to take at least one bite. Then if you don't like it, you can leave it on the plate. Also, we almost never fix special children's meals. She eats what we eat and isn't offered a different choice."
—*Jamie Hunley, San Diego, CA*

"Addie has finicky moments, especially with new foods. Once she tries a new food, she almost instantly takes to it, but getting her to try it can be difficult. What seems to work best is to introduce the new food to her without any pressure to eat it. The more times she sees the new food, the more likely she is to try it, especially if she sees my husband and I enjoying it over and over again. It took several months before she would even touch chicken, but with time and a little patience on our part, she finally took a bite and is now a poultry lover."
—*Chaya Reich, Los Angeles, CA*

"It depends on what it is. My oldest granddaughter will eat anything she hated two seconds before as long as it has barbeque sauce put on it. My son-in-law hates that because he likes to cook fancy food, but the important thing is that she eats."
—*Jeannette Eshbach, Roy, UT*

"Whatever I cook is what's for dinner. I don't cook a special meal for the kids—ever. I act as if I don't care what they eat, and it doesn't become a control issue."
—*Karen Sultan, Rockville, MD*

"Offer a variety of foods and realize that toddlers often don't eat much. Give them things to dip their food in. Some kids like certain textures and hate others. Don't make it an issue. Food is one of the three things that a child has total control over (the other two being potty training and sleeping)."
—*Brenda Brown, Kapolei, HI*

CHAPTER NINE

Child Care

Going back to work—or even just leaving your baby with a babysitter on occasion—is hard enough, but the transition is even harder when you're worried about whether the child care you have is good enough. It's worth the extra time and effort to take steps to prevent a problem in advance. This chapter covers our best tips for finding top-notch child care and making the transition easier.

Our Simple Five-Step Plan for Finding Great Child Care

1. Figure out which type of care that you'd prefer: nanny, au pair, mother's helper, in-home day care, or day care center.
2. Get referrals from friends, relatives, neighbors, acquaintances, your church, or synagogue.
3. Check out parenting fairs, newsletters, and referral services sponsored by MOMS Clubs, other parenting groups, or your own company.
4. Contact the National Resource Center for Health and Safety in Child Care at 800-598-5437, and Child Care Aware at 800-424-2246 or www.childcareaware.org for referrals and advice.
5. For a nanny or mother's helper, put an ad in a local paper or go to an agency.

"I think the best thing is to decide in advance what type of care would work best for you. My husband I decided while I was still pregnant that we would prefer a day care center to any other option. Lots of factors can go into this decision. For example, day care centers are more expensive than in-home child care. A nanny is expensive if you're hiring for only one child, but once you have more than one, a nanny actually becomes more economical (especially if you have more than two).

"If you choose the nanny or in-home care route, you need to consider backup child care for when your caregiver is sick.

"If your child is older, you need to consider his/her personality. For example, my son is extremely energetic and we don't feel he would do well with a nanny because he needs a lot more activity than a single person can provide (no matter how good that nanny is). He's also very social and likes being around lots of people. If I had a shy child, I may have given more thought to hiring a nanny."
— *Krisztina Rab, Naperville, IL*

"Network, network, network. Ask women at church, work, and in your neighborhood. My source has always been networking through church. Although two of the care providers I have used in the last eight years have not been members of my church, one was the daughter-in-law of an acquaintance, and another knew someone who knew someone. It seems to me when you ask these people, they become your champions, too, asking around and networking for you."
— *Dana Baedke, Chalfont, PA*

"We found our nanny by advertising in our local newspaper. After an initial phone call screen, we set up interviews with interested people. We were fortunate, as our nanny had cared for children of an associate of ours, so we felt confident that the reference was solid. Otherwise, we would have likely done a background check on her as well."
— *Sandy Tsao, M.D., Boston, MA*

"For a nanny, go with an agency. They check backgrounds, references, TB tests, etc., and if you are not happy with a particular nanny, you can interview another. For day care and in-home child care, get a list of licensed caregivers from your state and check each one out thoroughly. Go to the day care provider's home and spend time to see how the caregivers interact with the children. If you can get a referral, all the better."
—Missi Darnell, Acton, CA

"My first step was to call the Child Care Resource Center (I'm sure most cities have them). They put all of your information into the computer, your requirements for a center (maybe you want your child to be in a small home setting rather than a center with 150 kids, for example). They will give you a list of providers that meet your needs, what sort of training/certification they have, etc. Then you go and interview them."
—Tessica Reynolds, Salt Lake City, UT

"The place we use now was recommended by a woman in my postpartum exercise class and also by a coworker of my husband, who did not know each other outside of the day care center. This center did not advertise, so we never would have heard about it otherwise.

"But it's also worth attending fairs sponsored by local parents' groups, etc. We find our best nannies through a newsletter published by one of these parents' groups."
—Stacey Sklar, Oakland, CA

"First, begin as soon as you can. Most good day care centers will have a waiting list, so the sooner you are placed on the list, the better off you will be. The best way to find a good provider is through word of mouth. Ask your friends, neighbors, and relatives where their kids go and check those places out first."
—Donna Davidson, Weymouth, MA

"Look on your state's website for Protective and Regulatory Services. They have a listing of all licensed day cares and in-home sitters, and you can search by zip code. They also list all of the visits the state has made within the last few years and if there were any code violations."

—Eva Lindsey, Dallas, TX

EDITOR'S NOTE: This information, including state regulations and contact information is available on the National Resource Center for Health and Safety in Child Care website (http://nrc.uchsc.edu/parents.htm).

"I have found over the years that referral services are wonderful and often give you an idea of what to look for, but the best way I have found is to ask other parents. All of my day care situations have been found through a referral from another friend or parent. It is a very important decision, and I really needed to hear from other parents that their children have done well with a certain provider before I made that decision."

—Sarah Fox, Fort Collins, CO

Five Steps to Zeroing In on a Good Day Care Center or Day Care Home

1. Do phone interviews first, then visit the centers or day care homes in person—both at scheduled and unscheduled times.
2. Bring a friend with you.
3. Prepare a list of questions in advance, including questions about the hours, the policy on parents dropping in, the ratio of kids-to-caregivers (three-to-one is best for infants and six-to-one for toddlers), the schedule for the day, the experience of the staff, the cleanliness and safety of the environment, the policy on sick children, etc.
4. Observe how the caregivers interact with the children and how the children respond to them.
5. Go with your instincts.

"Look for kids who are happy and well-stimulated (not bored). Another thing to focus on is hygiene. Are the kids walking around with dirty/wet diapers, runny noses, etc.? Watch the teachers deal with an active child or a child doing something they are not supposed to. Is the teacher patient? Does she yell or spank? Look at the kids leaving at the end of the day. Are they excited to leave or do they want to stay?"
—Kris Pena, M.D., Ventura, CA

"If you can drop by without making an appointment, it's even better. When interviewing and touring, I would recommend taking someone with you. Chances are, they may notice things you don't. Take notes, take a list of questions with you. Follow up with the state department of health and safety to make sure they've never had any complaints and double check on their credentials. Make sure they haven't expired. Also, if they claim CPR/first-aid training, remember, regular CPR classes are much different than the one taught strictly for infants and kids."
—Tessica Reynolds, Salt Lake City, UT

"We looked at the following: a) ratio of staff-to-children (younger children need a lower ratio), b) how happy and well cared for the children seemed, c) adequate space and equipment for play (both inside and outside), d) training of the staff; some have fully licensed nursery schools or kindergartens, and e) before school and after school programs."
—Beverly Waxler, M.D., Chicago, IL

"Friendliness of the staff and cleanliness of the facility are big things to look for. I also paid attention to how the facility was decorated. Were the kids' paintings and pictures hanging up? Was the atmosphere warm and inviting to the kids? How were the kids who were already attending? Did they seem happy and did it look like they were having fun? A big thing for me is that you, as a parent, should be able to drop in at any time without any given notice to the staff."
—Donna Davidson, Weymouth, MA

"It is important to actually visit places with a list of features that make a center optimal. The American Academy of Pediatrics has a publication with such a list. A center that is licensed under the strictest codes is a plus. Policy should be spelled out, and an open door policy is imperative. If you can't come and go at anytime, don't leave your child there! If you breastfeed and will be sending breast milk, be sure that the center is familiar with storage and usage of breast milk. Interview the specific caregiver your child will interact with and make sure you feel comfortable with them. I brought my child with me several times to see how she reacted to the caregiver as well.

"The caregiver-to-child ratio is extremely important, especially with infants. Also, the center should be locked, and people should have to check children in and out with specific policies in relation to the procedure. A daily routine for feeding, changing, and developmentally appropriate activities should be in place and followed."
—*Claire Bienvenu, Slidell, LA*

"Look for happy children! When you walk in the door, are the children engaged and active or parked in front of a television? Licensure and accreditation are important, obviously, but a licensed center can still be very mediocre in terms of interaction."
—*Jessica Stygles, Toledo, OH*

"Talk to a lot of people and follow your instincts. If your gut reaction is negative, follow it. Don't feel like you have to rationalize or pinpoint exactly what doesn't feel right. Just keep looking until you feel good about your decision. Ask the provider a lot of questions. Visit when other children are present, and always ask where your baby will eat and sleep."
—*Lori Stussie, Lawrence, KS*

"I worked in a day care center, and I advise moms to look for cleanliness. That may sound obvious, but ask yourself this: If they don't bother to keep the front of the school and the 'lobby' area clean, how clean do you think they keep the more 'hidden' areas? Is someone at the front desk at all times? Look for sign-in books at the desk. Look for strong locks on the front door. Look for security cameras mounted at all exits. Is there a keypad with a secret code for entry? If so, ask how often they change the code. If they make you feel paranoid for asking, walk out. There is no such thing as too much paranoia when it comes to the safety of your child.

"Ask about health-related rules. Are kids sent home with a fever? Vomiting? What about the staff? Is there a nurse or trained aide on site? What are the policies regarding administering medication if needed? Are all staff members trained in infant/child CPR? Ask to see the CPR certificates. They should be placed in each employee's file.

"What are the cleaning procedures? Are changing tables sprayed and cleaned after every use? Are employees wearing disposable gloves for every diaper change? Are the toys sanitized daily? What about food? Is it provided, and if so, ask to see the food handler's permit.

"Watch to see how the caregivers interact with one another. Believe me, I've seen more than my fair share of catfights erupting (complete with cursing and even physical violence) between caregivers in front of the children!

"How long have most caregivers been there? Don't be afraid to ask them directly. It can be tough for little ones to be constantly adjusting to the presence of new people every week."
—*Jenna Haldeman, Portland, OR*

"I have used centers and now a nanny, and with both, I checked out all of my options by calling around first, then developing a list of questions and doing phone interviews. When I had it narrowed down, I went to see four to five centers.

"The American Academy of Pediatrics prints a good list of things to look for in a center. You can check their website at www.aap.org or in the book *Caring for Your Infant and Young Child* under the child care section.

"Seeing the place really gives you a good feel for it. Then, before my child started, I went a couple of times and just hung out for an hour or so to help the caregiver get to know my baby and to see what went on.

"Big red flags are places that don't let you visit, places that are negative about breastfeeding, and places that have safety violations that you can see are wrong."
—*Karen Wang, M.D., Wayne, PA*

"Talk to and visit at least three providers' homes or centers. Don't be afraid to ask strange, obvious, or controversial questions. Such as:

1. Do you hold the infant/child while they're having a bottle or prop the bottle up for them? (I actually asked this question after interviewing a day care provider who actually told me she props the bottle up—very bad.)
2. How do you handle a crying child who can't seem to be soothed?
3. How long do you let the child go before changing a diaper with a bowel movement? Are they changed on a schedule or as needed?
4. Do you help potty train?
5. What is the diapering routine? Do you use gloves? How do you dispose of the diapers?
6. What is your policy on spanking or discipline in any form?
7. Does the day care provider allow toy guns to be played with in her home?
8. Do you allow pumped breast milk? (Not generally an issue here in California, aka "granola state," but in some states, I've heard it's an issue.)
9. Are there any pets in the home? Are the pets current on shots? Have the pets ever attacked anyone?
10. Are there any smokers in the home?
11. Are you on a funded food program? (They require healthy eating and records to prove it.)
12. Does the provider have any children of her own? Ages? If applicable, have they ever been in trouble with the law (thinking molestation, child abuse, etc.)?

—*Karen Hurst, Roseville, CA*

How to Interview a Nanny or an Au Pair

1. Do phone interviews first, then schedule in-person interviews.

2. Ask about her experience, her own children, her availability, why she is a nanny, why she left her last job, how she will get to work, what her childhood was like, what her parenting philosophy is, how she will discipline your kids, and what she will do in various situations.

3. Always check references and do a background check.

4. Observe how she interacts with your child.

"Ask about past experiences and what the ages of the children were and what they liked and didn't like about their last jobs. Give them scenarios, such as, if my daughter falls and it might be serious, how will you handle it? If my two-year-old is having a tantrum, how will you handle it, etc."
—*Missi Darnell, Acton, CA*

"Ask for references. Get any permission legally required for a background check. Ask if they would object to a closed-circuit system in the place they would be caring for the child. (Even if you have no intention of installing one, the thought of being recorded will remain in the caregiver's head and will discourage any actions you would be upset over.) Ask what they would do in certain situations, for example, what if someone tried breaking in or what if the child suddenly became unconscious.

"Ask if they have any certifications in health, safety, or similar courses, like CPR. Ask about their future career and personal plans to get a feel for how seriously they take the responsibility of caring for children. Ask about their education and any other questions that help you get a feel for the candidate's character. Always ask about issues that are important to you: If, for example, you want your caregiver to reinforce your spiritual, health, or lifestyle beliefs, be sure to discuss them in an interview."
—*Angel Smith, Brooksville, FL*

"Ask what they expect in terms of benefits, what activities they would do with a child in a typical day, how they might handle an example emergency (give them a scenario like a fire in the kitchen or a child falling or something). Ask about their philosophy on discipline and when they might find it impossible to follow a parent's orders on something."
—*Karen Wang, M.D., Wayne, PA*

"We have been through interviews for au pairs and interviews for nannies, and the questions you ask are completely different. For the au pairs, we ask questions about their personal lives, . . . why they are coming to the U.S., what they do in their free time, etc. For the nannies that we have interviewed, we have asked them to describe a typical day for us—either from past experience or from what they see with our kids. We ask them basic questions about experience and certifications, needs for salary and hours.

"We also give them a scenario, such as, the boys are crying and our daughter needs to get to school, how would you handle that situation? What do you do when you get stressed? Who took care of you as a child? What was one great lesson you learned as a kid? Why do you want to be a nanny? What did you eat as a child? What would you feed the kids?"
—*Sarah Fox, Fort Collins, CO*

"Look at things like, is the nanny capable of caring for your child as he/she gets older, her background in child care, and past nanny experience. Does she have any children of her own, what are her other obligations, what is her availability, how flexible is her schedule, and is she willing to teach/nurture your child and not just babysit? Lastly, does it feel like a right match, personality-wise?"
—*Sandy Tsao, M.D., Boston, MA*

"You MUST do a background check. You need to ask them if they will allow you to do one. You should ask about their experience. Make sure they are CPR and first aid certified. I would ask for a copy of their driving record if they will transport your children anywhere. I would also ask where they see themselves in the next one to five years. You do not want to hire someone every college semester."

—*Tiffany Zimmer, Baltimore, MD*

"We asked:
1. What were her experiences/references?
2. Did she raise children of her own?
3. Would she cooperate with our approach to child care, including discipline? (We wanted to use time-outs and no spanking.)
4. Would she respect our religious beliefs by NOT teaching her own beliefs (which were different from our own) to our child?
5. Would she agree with our priorities: The child was the first priority (over light housekeeping duties)?"

—*Beverly Waxler, M.D., Chicago, IL*

Making the Transition

Going back to work requires a transition for you as well as your baby. Here's our best advice for making it as smooth as possible.

SEVEN WAYS TO EASE THE TRANSITION TO CHILD CARE FOR YOU AND YOUR BABY

1. Ease you and your baby into it, by having the nanny come or dropping your baby off at day care for just a few hours at first. Start this before you have to return to work.
2. Don't linger over good-byes.
3. Call to check up on him as often as you want.
4. Come home or drop in at the day care center unexpectedly.
5. Let yourself feel upset or scared, but don't let your child see it.
6. Have your husband do the drop-off, while you do the pick-up.
7. Connect with other working moms.

"Let the baby spend a little time with the caregiver before it is time for them to be with the caregiver daily. Drop the child off for an hour one day, two hours a few days later, and so on. It will help them get used to being away from mom and dad for a little while during the day."
—Tanya Rosario, Bronx, NY

"We had our nanny come and start taking care of our son two weeks before I had to go back to work. That way, I could show her around the house, our son could get used to another person, and my nanny and I could get comfortable with each other. This made the transition run smoothly for us."
—Sandy Tsao, M.D., Boston, MA

"If you feel the need to call and check in, do it. Make sure you get a detailed account of the baby's day. I found it extremely helpful when my day care provided me with a daily paper report stating when the baby slept, for how long, what they ate during the day, when the diaper was changed, etc."
—April McConnell, Birdsboro, PA

"Start with a couple of half days, if possible. For an infant, the transition is much easier than for the mom, but the baby may still react to the change in surroundings by not eating or sleeping well. Expect a few overtired evenings until your baby learns to nap at day care. Try to defer all evening housekeeping duties in the beginning, so you can just come home and cuddle or hold or nurse your baby. Order pizza, let the house get dirty, and skip social engagements until you are into somewhat of a routine (it takes a couple of weeks). The hardest transition is learning to get up, get the baby ready, get yourself ready, and get everyone out of the house and into day care before you have to be at work!"
—Diana Molavi, M.D., Baltimore, MD

"Let yourself be upset, but try to be happy and strong for your child. I think they have a harder time when you're upset. I have found with all three of my children they are fine and excited to go (or have the nanny take care of them). It is mom who has a hard time.

"What we ended up doing is that my husband does the morning drop-off, and I do the afternoon pick-up. This is much easier on everyone. I can leave before the kids wake up in the morning (for some reason, this creates less guilt), then I get the wonderful greeting at pick-up. The kids do much better when my husband drops them off. He doesn't have the same sense of guilt.

"It really helps to have close friends at work who are working moms. They understand what you are going through. You're happy to be back at work—and extremely guilty about that happiness—while at the same time, really, really missing the baby. I know I cried the first week that I left my daughter and the boys. I really needed that support group when I got to the office."

—Sarah Fox, Fort Collins, CO

"Visit as often as possible. Make your presence known. Take time to really talk with the caregivers at the end of the day, rather than just doing the grab and run. Always say thank you to the caregivers at the end of the day. It might not sound like much, but it means the world to them. When your kids see you treating the teacher with affection and respect, they are much more likely to do so as well."

—Jenna Haldeman, Portland, OR

CHAPTER TEN

SAVING MONEY

Nobody said having a kid was going to be cheap. But there are lots of ways to save money if you know a few tricks. Here are our favorites.

Our Number One, Ultimate Source for Saving Money on Baby Clothes, Gear, Books, Toys, and Just About Everything Else

eBay

"The best place to get most nursery essentials could easily be eBay. The selection is vast, and the quality (if you look specifically for 'new with tags' or 'new without tags' items) can be very high, while at the same time the prices are very reasonable."
—*Tracy Pritchard, Kyle, TX*

"EBay is the best for finding baby essentials at low cost. People sell a lot of things they never used, like baby clothes that were never worn because the baby grew out of them too fast. You can find awesome items at awesome prices. Make sure to add in the cost of shipping, though.

"You can put in your city in the search options (and check the Search Titles and Descriptions box) and find all of the items that are being sold in your area. Most sellers will let you pick up the item, which saves bundles on shipping!"
—*Eva Lindsey, Dallas, TX*

"EBay has practically new designer clothes for a fraction of the cost. For decor, I bought a big 8 x 10 antique Mother Goose book on eBay for $6, cut out the full-page illustrations and put them in chic, European-style frameless glass on the walls ($4 each). It looks FAB, and I can change the pictures as often as I like."
—*Gail Vold Greco, Minneapolis, MN*

"I buy most of my son's clothes on eBay. I can get almost new, name-brand clothes for almost nothing. My best buy was a group of eight brand-new outfits (still with the tags on) from The Children's Place for $30."
—*Sara Hammontree, Mountain Home, AR*

"You can find some really great deals on brand-new products. It saves time ordering from your computer. It saves gas, wear and tear on the car, potential accidents, you name it."
—*Colleen Bouchard, Bel Air, MD*

The Six Simplest Ways to Save Money on Nursery Essentials

1. Shop garage sales and consignment stores.
2. Borrow.
3. Shop the clearance sections of your favorite stores online.
4. Make curtains, bedding, and accessories yourself.
5. Comparison shop online.
6. Buy things that can grow with your baby.

"I was able to find our changing table for $10 at a garage sale. Scour them in neighborhoods if you are really in a cash crunch and you can find just about anything. Also, secondhand stores that cater specifically to baby furniture and clothes are a deal. You always want to check the durability of the furniture, however. Make sure shelves and legs are stable enough to use."
—*Lisa McDonald, Maitland, FL*

"Buy things that your baby can use as a toddler or even as a teen, such as furniture that you can add pieces to. Natural wood or white can really go a long way."
—*Andrea Suissa, Olney, MD*

"Shop consignment shops! We bought a changing table for $30 at a consignment shop. The next day, we happened to be at Babies R Us and saw the exact same table for $95! Also, borrow, borrow, borrow! They'll only be in the crib for a few years."
—*Daryl D'Angelo, Sewell, NJ*

"Shop garage sales, especially ones run by older people who just had a few items to use when the grandkids came over, because you can get the essentials cheaper, but in brand-new condition. I also recommend the clearance sales at BabyCenter.com because you can get new stuff cheap."
—*Ange Gregory, Stanwood, IA*

"BabyCenter.com and PotteryBarnKids.com both have great clearance sections."
—*Jenna Haldeman, Portland, OR*

"Consignment, consignment, consignment! A great website is www.kidsconsignmentguide.com. This website lists consignment sales for children all around the South. If you are not in the South, a simple search will hopefully pull up a similar website for your area. If you can purchase used matching furniture, that may give you the extra money you need to purchase the higher-priced bedding you so desperately want."
—*Dana Croy, Murfreesboro, TN*

EDITOR'S NOTE: Babyzone.com provides listings of local parenting resources, including consignment shops, all over the U.S., Canada, England, Scotland, and Australia. Resources for Ireland and Wales are coming soon.

"Go to resale shops. They are great. I went to one in Matthews called Once Upon a Child. They have a lot of great deals on

cribs, dressers, toys, and clothes. You can also check the sale ads in the classified section. Lots of people sell great baby stuff, like swings and car seats."
—*Debbie Clark, Charlotte, NC*

"I always go online and research the products I am interested in. I go to a variety of websites that carry the same products to try and get the best deal."
—*Desiree Bochman, Paradise, CA*

"I think the best investment for clothing and such is a built-in closet system. Ours was under $400 and has drawers, shelves, a rod for hanging, etc. (You can do it yourself for much cheaper though. Home Depot will cut wire shelving to size free of charge.) I can fit all of my son's stuff in there, including extra diapers, stored clothes for two years (past, present, and future), extra sheets, blankets, user manuals, extra stroller parts, Pack 'n Play, breast pump, etc. You don't get the wasted space that just one long rod gives (since kids' clothes only take up about a foot down from that), and it costs little more than buying a dresser. The room has just a crib and changing table, which leaves a lot more room for playing and toys."
—*Kari Rydell, Ladera Ranch, CA*

Nine Clever Strategies to Avoid Overpaying for Baby Gear, Clothes, Books, and Toys

1. Don't just clip coupons; buy them (and formula rebate checks, too) in quantity on eBay and other online mom swap boards.
2. Request coupons and samples from baby product manufacturers directly.
3. Join a local MOMS Club (www.momsclub.org) or other support group for moms and swap outgrown baby clothes, products, furniture, toys, and books with other members.
4. Shop at the semiannual Mothers of Twins Club

(www.nomotc.org) baby sale (you don't need to be a member).

5. Check BabyCenter's bargain-hunting bulletin board for good deals and great sales.

6. Use websites like Epinions.com and Dealtime.com to search for the best deals on everything from car seats to nursing pillows.

7. Buy used books from your local library.

8. Shop at BabyCatalog.com for car seats, strollers, toys, feeding supplies, etc. at the guaranteed lowest price.

9. Shop the clearance sections of top-name stores like Lands' End, Pottery Barn Kids, The Gap, and Old Navy online. Lands' End also has a special On the Counter section where limited-quantity items are put up for sale on Saturday and marked down by 25 percent each subsequent day until there are none left.

"I've found car seats at BabyCatalog.com for $40 cheaper than Babies R Us and no shipping charges!"
—Kris Rivas, Denver, CO

"Check your area for a local Mothers of Multiples group. This organization holds two annual baby sales where twin moms will be selling clothing and baby gear that is practically unused."
—Jenna Haldeman, Portland, OR

"I use Epinions.com. They rate gear and search the web for the best prices and compare for you."
—Tiffany Zimmer, Baltimore, MD

"Our library is a great source for children's books, since they sell their used books for 50 cents each. Cheap baby toys are everywhere: Empty food boxes (cereal, pasta, tea, sugar) are colorful blocks; a bag of fabric scraps is a great source of tactile entertainment; plastic measuring cups, spoons, and Tupperware are

old classics; and a big shoe box full of duplicate photos, Christmas and birthday cards and Home Depot paint swatches makes for endless amusement."
—*Diana Molavi, M.D., Baltimore, MD*

"You can buy formula [rebate] checks and diaper coupons in quantity on eBay. Call all those baby companies and tell them you love their products, but things are really expensive. Then ask if they can send any money-saving coupons."
—*Andrea Suissa, Olney, MD*

"I shop almost exclusively online for clothes and only look in the 'sale' and 'clearance' sections at OldNavy.com and Gap.com, etc. I never see the newest stuff, so I am not tempted to buy anything that's not on sale! I also use points from my credit cards (I have a Yahoo Visa and an American Express) that let me get gift certificates to tons of stores—Toys R Us, Old Navy, Gap, Target, Amazon.com, etc."
—*Kari Rydell, Ladera Ranch, CA*

"One of my favorite sites on the Internet is the 'bargain-hunting' board on BabyCenter (www.BabyCenter.com/bbs/5465). Parents share any great offers and sales they have seen with other parents. There is always at least one great thing to read on that site each day, ranging from great advice to a wonderful free sample available to parents. It's a great resource for looking for ways to save money."
—*Heather French, Fishers, IN*

Our Nine Best Tips for Saving Money on Child Care and Babysitting

1. Ask family members to babysit.
2. Have dad stay home with the kids.
3. Work opposite shifts, so one parent can always be home with the kids.
4. Ask for discounts if you have more than one child in day care.

5. Share a nanny or babysitter.
6. Hire an au pair.
7. Participate in a flexible spending program for child care.
8. Set up a swapping or co-op arrangement with friends whereby you trade off babysitting each other's kids.
9. Check into Moms' Day Out programs, often sponsored by local churches or governments.

"My husband and I arranged special work schedules: I work weekdays, from 8 a.m. to 5 p.m., while my husband works Saturday through Wednesday from 3 p.m. to 11 p.m. He stays with our daughter all day Thursdays and Fridays, and on the other weekdays, since both our parents reside in the same town, they babysit her (free of charge!) for the two hours between 3 and 5 p.m. until I get home. We realize we're very fortunate—not everyone has families so near or careers so accommodating. It saves us from costly day care and it's a wonderful way for the grandparents to spend quality time with their granddaughter."
—*Elizabeth Hildebrand, Greenville, PA*

"The best way to find a good, reliable child care provider whom you know you can trust to love and care for your child as much as you would is to turn to their father. I can't think of a luckier child in the world than one taken care of by a loving, stay-at-home daddy. If mommy makes the most money, as I do, but day care scares you, I would encourage you to explore this option.

"This is not to say it is easy or that all men would be able to handle it, but it is worth considering. My husband loves his new and much more challenging, but rewarding, career as a full-time dad. I go to work each day knowing that my child is safe and secure and that he is being shaped by the most wonderful man in the world. When I get home, I have the luxury of being 100 percent mom, no dinner to cook or errands to run."
—*Sarah Hallberg, M.D., Indianapolis, IN*

"My father-in-law lives with us. Having family is obviously the most convenient and economical solution. Another thing we have done

is provide room and board for a full-time college student in exchange for help with the kids. This has worked out great—she has become more like an addition to the family than an employee."
—Rebecca Smondrowski, Gaithersburg, MD

"Since we had three children and they were all young, we used an au pair for two years. Au pairs live in your home, and, in exchange for room and board, they watch the kids. We had a great experience and enjoyed having live-in child care, especially with twins. It was really nice when the kids were sick to know they could stay home in good hands, and you could go to work. Best of all, the au pair program is cheaper than day care (when you have more than one child). There are two main agencies that help and some great resources of local parents who have gone through the program. Even in Fort Collins, we have about fifteen to twenty families in the au pair program."
—Sarah Fox, Fort Collins, CO

"When we found out we were going to have child number two, we did the math, added up child care costs and realized that in the end, all we had was $100 extra bucks a week—maybe— and a lot of added stress because both parents were working. As a result, my husband quit his job and stayed home with our two kids. That was thirteen years ago. Since then, we've had three more children, he's still home and successfully raising healthy, good, honor roll students."
—Dodi Kingsfield, Forestville, NY

"In order to save on child care, I work an adjusted work week— 9.5 hour days four days a week—so we only need child care for four days. My mother and sister are able to keep my son one of the four days, so we are only having to pay for three days of care, and my son gets to spend time with his grandmother and aunt.

"As for date nights, we are blessed to live close to both of our parents and my sister, so we are usually able to find a loving relative to keep an eye on our son so we can get some couple time."
—Heather French, Fishers, IN

TO CONTRIBUTE TO THE NEXT EDITION,
VISIT WWW.GALLAGHERGUIDE.COM

"My primary child care provider offers a family discount. When a family has more than one child in her care, she reduces the fees. Also, she reduces fees if you bring food to her. When I get really good deals at the grocery store, I bring the extra to her and pay less for my day care."
—*Colleen Grace Weaver, San Lorenzo, CA*

"We rarely go out anywhere where we can't take our child. But if we do, we trade off with other parents. If a bunch of parents want to have a childless evening together, we sometimes have all the kids stay at one house and all the adults at a very nearby house. We have the older kids (ten to fourteen) arrange games and activities and all the parents take turns spending a few minutes at the kid house, so there's always an adult present, but the kids entertain themselves. This only works if you socialize with your close neighbors and have pretty well-behaved kids, but the kids love it and so do the parents.

"Our local YMCA also offers Parents' Night Out at least once a month. They will entertain a limited number of children for about $15 for several hours."
—*Jamie Hunley, San Diego, CA*

"My husband and I have always worked opposite shifts. We believe in one of us always being there for our kids, and it certainly saves on child care, especially if you're paying for more than one child."
—*Bobbi Annal, Spokane, WA*

The Single Easiest, Most Effortless Way to Save for College

Join Upromise (www.upromise.com)

"I am signed up with Upromise (www.upromise.com) where a portion of the things I buy from grocery stores and various brick and mortar and online stores gets saved to an account. This account is then deposited quarterly into my daughter's 529 plan

[state-sponsored tuition savings plan]. If you're going to spend money at these stores anyway, why not get some money back to put toward your child's education?"
—*Karen Hurst, Roseville, CA*

"I have a Upromise account for each of my sons, and I sent an e-mail to all my relatives asking them to register. I don't expect this will cover a year of college or anything, but maybe it will help with books."
—*Lori Stussie, Lawrence, KS*

"We have a Upromise account, which we have our credit cards and grocery store cards tied to. When we purchase from participating stores or restaurants, we get a percentage rebate. Upromise also allows you to link your 529 plan to your Upromise account and transfer the money into it."
—*Dianna Schisser, Frederick, MD*

CHAPTER ELEVEN

GETTING ORGANIZED

T he word "multitasking" was probably invented by a mom. Sometimes it seems you need twelve arms to do everything you have to do in a day. That's why we've become experts at doing things quickly and efficiently. This chapter reveals our best tricks for organizing our homes, our time, and our lives.

Saving Time in the Morning

The morning rush can be more stressful in your home than it is on a major highway if you and/or the kid(s) have to go somewhere and you aren't organized. Here are the best ways to get everything done smoothly and efficiently.

OUR TOP SIX TIPS FOR
MAKING THE MORNING RUSH GO SMOOTHLY

1. Do as much as possible the night before.
2. Get ready before the kids get up.
3. Share the workload.
4. Shower at night.
5. Allow more time than you need to get ready.
6. Streamline your routine as much as possible by cutting your hair or forgoing makeup.

"Make lunch the night before, get plenty of help from your husband, and most of all, get up really early so that mornings aren't rushed."
—Linda Linguvic, New York, NY

"I often have to leave before my daughter wakes up in the morning, which leaves my husband to get our little girl ready. To make things easier on him (and me, so I don't have to see her in odd outfits), I put all of the parts of an outfit (socks included) in a big Ziploc bag as I'm folding and putting away laundry. That way, all he has to do is pick up a bag, and all the pieces are there."
—Chelsea Hamman, M.D., Providence, NC

"The diaper bag is always packed and my husband's lunch is made the night before. I allow plenty of time, and I am proud to say I have still never been late for anything, even with twins."
—Patricia Arnold, Westford, MA

"I take a shower at night and always plan what I am going to wear before I get out of bed. If I stand in front of the closet, it takes too long. I also always watch the weather to be sure to dress appropriately."
—Shelly Huggins, Bel Air, MD

"Always get up before your children! I try to get up early enough to have some quiet time, grab a cup of coffee, exercise, shower, and dress before my children get up. Since my oldest is an early riser, I have to get started pretty early in order to accomplish this. On days when I am not able to, I find myself running two steps behind my children. I need that head start on the day and time to collect myself. Once I'm on track, I'm better able to tend to the needs of my children and oversee the things they are doing. It also leaves me more quality time to spend with them. It makes for an all-around better day."
—Angela Snodgrass, Meridian, ID

"I usually prepare the night before. I purchase Lunchables or sometimes I call the deli and let them know I'm on my way to drop my kids off to school. Lunch is usually ready by the time I stop by."
—*Dawn Kirnon, M.D., New York, NY*

THE SEVEN MOST VALUABLE TOOLS FOR A TIME-CRUNCHED MOM

1. Online bill payment
2. Palm Pilot
3. Quicken or Microsoft Money
4. Online calendar
5. Grocery delivery service
6. Housekeeper or maid service
7. Flylady system (www.Flylady.com)

"I live for my Palm! I have everything in there, and it's small enough to throw in my purse or diaper bag. It's great for scheduling doctor's appointments, as you always have your family calendar with you. You can make lists in there while you are waiting somewhere. It's a lot safer than a piece of paper that can get lost. All my phone numbers are in there, so I can make phone calls from the car when I don't have my son with me and can talk quietly."
—*Becky Messerli, Chesterfield, MI*

"We sometimes use grocery delivery services. Getting to the supermarket with two kids can be very unpleasant, and it saves us over an hour of miserable time at the store. Also, getting heavy, bulky items delivered to our house (such as diapers) is a real bonus. If you order enough, delivery is often free!"
—*Stacey Sklar, Oakland, CA*

"I use Microsoft Money to handle finances because it is easy to show my husband where the money goes, which keeps him aware of our spending limits. I also use my Yahoo calendar to schedule EVERYTHING, from meals, appointments and due dates to my basal body temperature and prescription refill dates. I love the fact that I can access my schedule away from home. All I need is the Internet, which is widely available.

"There is a site called www.Flylady.com that saved my sanity while I was pregnant, separated, working full-time, and raising an eight-year-old and an eighteen-month-old. It teaches you how to organize your life and home so you have more time. It is a phenomenal organization that offers so much support! I make supply lists that I put on the inside of each cabinet door with a list of necessary items, and when something runs out, we just put a check on the list next to the item so we know to pick it up the next shopping trip. I also use this trick in the bathrooms and laundry room."

—*Angel Smith, Brooksville, FL*

"I pay bills like the car payment, insurance, phone bill, etc. with their online bill payment options. It saves me the time of sitting down and writing out checks. Plus, you get the confirmation as soon as you click send, so you don't have to worry about if the check made it there or not.

"When it comes to lists, I plan out a menu for each two-week pay period. Then I write down a list of all the groceries I will need. This way, meals are preplanned, all the food we need is in the house, and I don't have to make last-minute runs to the grocery store to get things I forgot."

—*Sara Hammontree, Mountain Home, AR*

"We pay all of our bills online or through automatic drafting. I hired a housekeeper to come in and clean twice a week. She is a lifesaver. And I write everything down in my day planner, since it goes everywhere with me."

—*Deborah Theriault, Norfolk, VA*

"I do everything possible online. Banking, bill paying, shopping, etc. It has cut the number of errands I need to run way down. I also correspond as much as possible by e-mail because I can do it when it's convenient for me. Taking care of our finances is

greatly simplified by using Quicken software to keep track of our expenses."
—*Jamie Hunley, San Diego, CA*

So What Do You Do with All that Stuff?

Remember when it took less than ten minutes to clean up the clutter around your house in the evening? Then you had kids. And the older they get, the more they accumulate. When it comes to finding a place to store it all, we look for options that let us stow it when we don't want to use it, but allow us to easily find it when we do.

**OUR FAVORITE WAYS TO
STORE KIDS' TOYS AND STUFF**

1. Rubbermaid plastic storage containers
2. Baskets
3. Toy bin/shelf combo units
4. Hammocks for stuffed animals

"I use plastic containers, labeled and sorted, each with a certain type of toy in them. I recommend them because they're easy to stack and store, easy for a child to manage, and children learn sight recognition of words when checking the toy labels."
—*Valerie Downs, Altoona, PA*

"I just use Rubbermaid bins and try to sort the toys within the bins. The kind that slide under the bed are ideal, because it's an instant clean room!"
—*Megan Martin, Crystal Lake, IL*

"In the first few months of my daughter's life, I thought all the stuffed animals were so cute and cuddly. However, as the months have passed, they have become not only dust magnets, but they take up so much space. We recently purchased a 'pet net,' which hangs from the ceiling and holds up to sixty stuffed animals!"
—*Billie Smith, Turpin, OK*

"Baskets, baskets, and more baskets! They sort, they stack, and they store almost anything. Plus, they look good. I think that a real key to being organized is taking the time to get organized. If you make sure everything has a place, then it is easier to keep things where they belong."
—Rebecca Smondrowski, Gaithersburg, MD

"We have several cubby shelves and baskets that we got from Ikea. It's easy for them to put all their toys in the baskets, and the shelving is attractive enough, so it looks great."
—Colleen Bouchard, Bel Air, MD

"I store them in plastic bins. They are great, especially the clear ones. They look nice and neat, and my kids know where everything belongs because they can see through the clear plastic. Rubbermaid makes a lot of different colors and styles. I like the ones that have drawers."
—Alejandra Dozal, El Paso, TX

Getting Stains Out of Kids' Clothes

There's nothing cuter than a ten-month-old covered from head to toe in spaghetti sauce. But once you've taken a picture and plopped the munchkin in the bath, you're still faced with the problem of getting the clothes clean.

We recommend treating stains as soon as possible. Even if you don't plan on washing the item right way, you can pretreat the stain. Also, never put clothes in the dryer if the stain hasn't come out. Once they are dried, the stain is set.

BEST STAIN-FIGHTING PRODUCT

OxiClean

"I have found that OxiClean is the only thing that works. The toughest stains I have had are ones on her bibs that have set for

a while. I soak them in OxiClean (sometimes overnight) and the garment comes out looking brand new. It does not bleach."
—*Becky Gaston, Owensboro, KY*

"OxiClean seems to get stains out of almost anything. For really bad stains, you can make a paste with it, rub it into the stain and allow it to sit. The stain will be gone without a trace in no time.

"My friend's daughters have a cream-colored carpet in their bedroom. It has had food, Kool-Aid, crayons, basically everything on it, and OxiClean has managed to get it all out and leaves the carpet looking like new. It also worked on a crayon mishap in a dryer."
—*Kelly Harden, Ft. Hood, TX*

"I am a huge fan of OxiClean. It gets most food stains out without hurting the fabric, and I can use it for odd jobs around the house. The other day, I used it to get beet juice out of a pair of Samantha's pants, and that night, it removed a huge red wine stain on the couch when I accidentally spilled my glass."
—*Jennifer Weintraub, Dallas, TX*

"I have found that all of the children's stain lifters are basically all just a bunch of hype. I find that OxiClean works the very best, and if that won't take it out, nothing will!"
—*Rebecca Harper, Gaston, SC*

Storing and Displaying Kids' Artwork

Just as the plethora of baby gear begins to clear (the Exersaucer goes to a neighbor, the high chair gets put away, the crib gets stored downstairs), your kid hits preschool. Then you are inundated with artwork. When it's your first child, and the first time you see what your little genius has made, you are overcome with pride. You proudly display the blue scribble on your refrigerator, reflecting on your prodigy's potential future as an artist.

Several months later, when your refrigerator is buried behind stacks of construction-paper drawings, and you can no longer find the handle on the door, you begin to consider other options. Here are our recommendations.

EIGHT CLEVER WAYS TO MANAGE THE DELUGE OF KIDS' ARTWORK

1. Store special artwork that you want to save in a box or Rubbermaid container. Be sure to put the child's name and the date on the back of the artwork.
2. Display it on a bulletin board or magnetic board.
3. Use clothespins to clip it to a clothesline that you've tacked onto the wall.
4. Put it on the refrigerator and rotate it every week.
5. Store it in a box until you have a lot, then take it all out, put it on display, and take your child's picture standing in front of it.
6. Display it in a shadow box frame or special art frame that can be changed easily.
7. Scan special pieces into the computer to resize and print out as you like.
8. Give it to the grandparents.

"We made a magnetic board in our playroom. We bought magnetic paint (found in specialty hardware stores only, not the big chains), painted a bright color over it, and then framed it with molding painted in another bright color. Ours measures about 5' x 10', so it becomes a focal point of the room. All of their projects get put on the wall with magnets that we collect wherever we go."
—Debbie Ezrin, Gaithersburg, MD

"The first thing is to date it and make sure the child's name is on it. I didn't do that with my first two. Now, when going through their things, I'm not always sure whose is whose."
—Desiree Bochman, Paradise, CA

"I hang it on the refrigerator for one month, then take a picture of all of it and put it into the scrapbook."
—Deshawn Anderson-Drew, Apopka, FL

"Frame one to two pieces in a cheap wooden frame painted to match the child's room. Choose a frame that is easy to take apart, with or without glass. Then change the pictures each week or when they get a new art project.

"I also hung a piece of string (you could use ribbon to make it cuter) on one of the walls of the playroom, by pinning it on both ends and in the middle to make a swag. I clip all art projects to it, so the kids can see them. This communicates that their creativity and projects are important. At the same time, it keeps your refrigerator and the rest of the house less cluttered."
—*Kerith Leffler, Morristown, NJ*

"Ikea makes a cute clothesline wall-hanging with tiny clothespins. Hang the art on this, and rotate every month or so."
—*Kris Pena, M.D., Ventura, CA*

"I have a large Rubbermaid container that I have labeled with her age, and I make sure to save the artwork that we all liked the best. I also will scan her artwork into the computer (after placing her name and date on the bottom in pen), then shrink it down to about a 3 x 3-inch image, and print it out and place that on a magnetic sheet.

"They make magnetic paper for ink jet printers that you can buy at any office supply store, however, what I use is a little different. You can purchase a magnetic sheet that is 8.5 x 11 inches from Target (in the photo department). One side is the magnetic side and the other side has paper on it that you can peel off to reveal a sticky surface. I cut a square from the sheeting that is a bit larger than her artwork. I then peel off the paper, and I position the artwork on the sticky side of the magnet and smooth it down. Just trim off the overage and you're set. Instant refrigerator art that's a wonderful keepsake!"
—*Colleen Bouchard, Bel Air, MD*

"Fridges are great for displaying. I have also hung string across the ceiling of the playroom and I hang work from this with clothes-pegs."
—*Rachel Hampton-Saint, Kent, England*

"Decoupage it onto a wall or iron onto a blanket. To iron on, first scan the artwork into your computer. Then get special iron-on transfer paper (sold at Wal-Mart or craft stores) and put that in your printer. Print out the artwork, and just iron on like any other transfers. You can make a carrying bag or T-shirts as well. They look really nice."
—Valerie Downs, Altoona, PA

"One of the neatest ideas I have ever seen is to mount fairly large frames directly on the wall. You take a frame—no glass or backing—and hang it on the wall. You can then hang children's artwork on the wall (inside the frame) with the white tacky stuff that doesn't damage the walls. (It comes in little blocks; you can break off a piece and knead it, then stick things on the wall without any permanent damage to the wall.) Since it is not really framed, you can change artwork frequently, yet it really makes each piece look very special."
—Sally Farrington, Fayetteville, NC

Saving Time in the Evening

They don't call it the "witching hour" for nothing. That one to two hour time span right before dinner is always crazy when you have little ones. You have to get dinner on the table. You have to clean up the clutter in the house and put away your own belongings from the car or work. You have to make sure they've done their homework, and prepared what they need for the next day. And you have to do it all before they melt down from exhaustion (or drive you insane!). Here are our best solutions for handling the evening rush.

FIVE RECOMMENDATIONS FOR
TAKING THE EDGE OFF THE EVENING RUSH

1. Follow a routine.
2. Share the workload.
3. Cook in bulk, use the slow cooker, and buy premade foods, such as cooked rotisserie chicken.

4. Start preparing dinner earlier in the day.

5. Skip the bath.

"My husband is 'the bath man.' While I clean up the kitchen after dinner, he gives our four- and two-year-olds a bath. They really enjoy that time with him, and it allows me to have a few minutes of quiet."
—*Kimberly Mercurio, M.D., Downers Grove, IL*

"I do as much dinner prep when my oldest is in school and my younger one is napping as I can."
—*Susan Tachna, Palo Alto, CA*

"When making meat, I always cook enough for two to three meals. I cook enough chicken so we can eat chicken breasts one night, make stuffed chicken pasta shells the next, and chicken wraps the third night."
—*Tamara Prince, Oshawa, Ontario, Canada*

"Prepare food in advance. I used to do all my cooking on Sundays. I worked and wanted to just be able to heat up something fast."
—*Linda Linguvic, New York, NY*

"Some days if we're home early and the kids need a bath, I'll bathe them at 4 p.m. before dinner instead of waiting until after when everyone is starting to have a meltdown. I like to keep a few prepared dinners in the freezer for those nights when you don't have time to cook."
—*Kate Steiman, Toms River, NJ*

"I have found that Crock-Pot cooking helps ease dinner pressures. It's easy to throw things in a Crock-Pot, plug it in, and know that dinner will be ready when you get home."
—*Hannah Johnson, M.D., Elmhurst, IL*

"The hour before dinner tends to be very hectic—calming down from the day and coming in the house grubby from play takes up a good portion of dinner preparation time. What I do is prepare dinner in the middle of the day (when feasible). I enjoy this 'quiet' time of the day preparing our family meals. Lots of Crock-Pot meals, soups, egg noodle dishes, salads—things I only have to reheat just before sitting down to the meal.

"When I do it this way, the hour before mealtime is used for cleaning up the living area, organizing homework assignments, breaking up sibling arguments, etc., supervising children's chores, bringing laundry to the laundry room, etc. When we do sit down, the kids are clean, the house is tidy, the meal is prepared stress-free, and Daddy comes home to a loving, warm family dinner."
—*Lori Burgess, Bingham, ME*

Getting Dinner on the Table Fast

The biggest part of the evening rush is getting dinner ready before the kids melt down. Here are our favorite time-saving recipes.

FAST AND EASY RECIPES FOR
WHEN YOU ARE IN THE MOOD FOR A QUICKIE

"Chop a half a zucchini, ½ cup of carrots, and ½ cup of broccoli. Put it in a pot with ½ cup of orzo. Add enough water to cover. Bring to a boil and cook until the orzo is done. Drain, add a couple of tablespoons of butter (more if you would like), ½ cup of parmesan cheese, and a chopped cooked chicken breast. Yummy."
—*Patricia Arnold, Westford, MA*

"Sometimes I make a chicken and rice casserole: rice, chicken broth, and chicken dumped into a casserole dish and baked for 45 minutes at about 375 degrees. Sometimes I make chicken and stuffing casserole. Sometimes I throw frozen broccoli and a can of cream of mushroom soup in a casserole dish, then toss on some seasoned chicken, bake, and voila! Chicken and veggies. This is also good with frozen spinach. To make this really good (and a little more fattening) I put in some shredded cheese. An-

other easy chicken dish (and it's low fat) is to marinate the chicken in fat free honey dijon dressing all day (glass dish in the fridge), then coat it in corn flake crumbs and bake at 425 degrees for 20 minutes. Easy and delicious."
—*Beth Miller, Novato, CA*

"I am the queen of quick cooking. I like meals that are quick and call for ingredients that you normally keep on hand, like: Crock-Pot Pork Chops. You need two cans of cheddar cheese soup (or any kind of soup you like, such as cream of mushroom, etc.), two soup cans of milk, potatoes, thinly sliced pork chops, and salt and pepper.

"Important: Brown the pork chops for a few minutes on each side. This must be done or they will leave nasty stuff in your Crock-Pot. Peel and slice potatoes. Mix soup and milk together with a wire wisk. Put potatoes, pork chops, and soup into Crock-Pot. Make sure soup mix is enough to cover everything. If not, add more milk. Stir everything up. Add salt and pepper or I usually add Lawry's Seasoning Salt to mine. Cook on low all day. The pork chops are so tender, they just fall apart."
—*Brandy Charles, Tulsa, OK*

"I take one pound browned ground beef, one box of Velveeta Shells & Cheese (cooked per directions), ½ cup sour cream, salt, pepper, chili powder (optional), and combine all the ingredients for a creamy version of chili mac."
—*Keli Loveland, Bartlett, TN*

"Chicken and gravy or beef tips and gravy over pasta."
—*Karen Haas, Laurel, MD*

"I throw chicken breasts or thighs, a jar of salsa, a package of taco powder seasoning, ½ to 1 cup of water, a 15-ounce can of black beans, and a 15-ounce can of kidney beans into the Crock-Pot and cook all day long. When I get home, I use my rice cooker to make 1½ cups cooked rice, which I throw into the Crock-Pot after it's cooked. Then I top it with shredded Mexican cheese mix."
—*Michele Carlon, M.D., Chicago, IL*

"You can mix together whatever is in the fridge and serve it over pasta with frozen veggies and it seems like a good, home-cooked meal. Other than the traditional tomato-based sauces, I've used cooked chicken and broccoli with a little oil and garlic, ground beef and peppers, and just about any type of meat/fish/poultry with a cream of mushroom soup. You're limited only by your imagination and your kids' tastes.
—Julia Wonderling, Philadelphia, PA

"Broiled salmon in teriyaki sauce with pineapple. Marinate the salmon in teriyaki sauce and broil seven to nine minutes on each side with pineapple. Goes great with rice and asparagus."
—Eliza Chin, M.D., Piedmont, CA

"Pasta with spaghetti sauce and cottage cheese mixed in. Nice protein and calcium boost."
—Sarah Pletcher, East Lansing, MI

"Chicken and Rice. Preheat oven to 375 degrees. In a 13 x 9-inch baking dish, melt 1 stick of butter. Pour the butter over 1½ cups of raw long grain rice. Add salt and pepper to taste. Place about 5 boneless skinless chicken breasts on top of the rice. Sprinkle one package of Lipton's Onion Soup Mix over everything. Pour 3 cups of water over this. Cover tightly with foil and bake 1½ hours. You can double the recipe and put one pan in the freezer for a later date. It's also great reheated."
—Traci Bragg, M.D., Jacksonville, FL

"Rebecca's One Dish Pasta Casserole. 1 bag of pasta (any kind will do; I like rotini), 1 pound of ground meat, your choice (beef, chicken, etc.), 1 large jar of tomato sauce or 1 medium-small jar of sauce and 1 can of tomatoes, 1 onion, chopped mushrooms (canned or fresh; canned is fastest; if fresh, then chopped), frozen veggies (corn is our family favorite), grated cheese.

"Fry ground meat and onions while boiling water. Add mushrooms to the fry pan in the last few minutes. (I have found that boiling the water in the kettle is a lot faster than waiting for it to boil in the pot if you are in a big hurry.) When the water is boiling, add the pasta and frozen veggies. Cook until the pasta is done. Strain. In pot or CorningWare dish, mix pasta mixture, cooked meat mixture, and tomato products. Stir well. Sprinkle cheese over top. Place in a preheated 350-degree oven until the cheese is melted and sauce is warm."

—*Rebecca Curtis, Oshawa, Ontario, Canada*

CHAPTER TWELVE

ENTERTAINMENT

You don't need to spend a lot of money to entertain your baby. Many of the most exciting and stimulating toys for babies are plain old household objects, such as measuring cups (great for stacking), pots and pans (what baby doesn't love to make noise?), your keys, and, everyone's favorite, the remote control. Of course, you may not want your baby teething on your car keys or your remote control, but we're just talking about what they'd *want* to play with, not what you'd *let* them play with.

Toys

When we're shopping for toys, safety is our first criterion. That means no small parts, long cords, or strings that can be wrapped around baby's neck. We also look for toys that are durable, colorful, and engaging.

OUR THREE FAVORITE FIRST TOYS FOR BABY

1. Activity gym, such as the Gymini
2. Rattle
3. Mobile

"I love the activity gyms. With my oldest son, it was a very simple Sesame Street plastic gym, and now with my baby, it is a softer

version. It stimulates them visually and physically, but isn't loud or flashy. I think it is important for them to have time to make their own entertainment, rather than bells and whistles too early on."
—*Lisa Brooks, Butler, PA*

"The activity arch is great for keeping babies' attention and useful during tummy time if it has a play mat that goes with it, too."
—*Kelly Harden, Ft. Hood, TX*

"I recommend a soft rattle with chimes or different textures. On the bigger side, a Gymini mat is fantastic."
—*Karen Wang, M.D., Wayne, PA*

"I recommend mobiles, especially the ones with black/white/red designs. The music is soothing, the images are stimulating, and it usually keeps infants entertained and happy for a period of time."
—*Kris Pena, M.D., Ventura, CA*

OUR ABSOLUTE FAVORITE BRAND OF BABY TOYS

Fisher-Price

"I love Fisher-Price toys. If I had millions, I would buy every toy they have. They are imaginative, fun, educational, and made according to age."
—*Alisa Norris, Plano, TX*

"I like Fisher-Price baby toys. They're sturdy, and they are always improving them. Plus, they're really good about replacing lost parts."
—*Amy Kobler, Buffalo, NY*

"I like Fisher-Price because they make some of the classic toys, and they are known for safety."
—*Krystal Johnston, M.D., Manistee, MI*

"Fisher-Price is affordable and has very innovative products for kids."
—*Sandy Tsao, M.D., Boston, MA*

"Fisher-Price toys are sturdy, creative, educational, and my daughter loves them!"
—*Kris Pena, M.D., Ventura, CA*

Books

Experts recommend reading to baby from birth, and we couldn't agree more. At first, your baby may do little more than use books for teething toys, but eventually, the lyrical language and wonderful pictures of these books will get through, and he'll be able to truly enjoy them.

THE FIRST FIVE BOOKS TO BUY FOR BABY

1. *Goodnight Moon* by Margaret Wise Brown
2. Anything by Dr. Seuss
3. Anything by Sandra Boynton, especially *The Going to Bed Book*
4. A Touch and Feel Book
5. *Brown Bear, Brown Bear, What Do You See?* or any other book by Eric Carle

"*Goodnight Moon* has been Orion's favorite book for bedtime. It was a part of his routine for a while, and now he goes to bed 'reading' alone after I read it to him. I also love all the Dr. Seuss books."
—*Alisa Norris, Plano, TX*

"I recommend the classics—*Where the Wild Things Are, The Very Hungry Caterpillar,* and *Goodnight Moon.* I like the generational aspect of these books and think they make for good bonding for parent and child. Parents often remember how much they enjoyed them when they were children. I also like that they don't have characters that are marketed to parents and get kids started on character 'buy, buy, buy' obsessions."
—*Jennifer Brannon, Huntington Beach, CA*

"All of my children love *The Foot Book* by Dr. Seuss. We began reading it to our firstborn when he was about six months old and have read it to our other children as well. We played with their feet while we read it, and they still love it. They are seven, six, and three now."
—*Kristen Math, Sartell, MN*

"I love *Good Night Gorilla* and *Goodnight Moon*. The repetition in *Goodnight Moon* is very soothing for kids, and they love to see the beautiful pictures."
—*Karen Sultan, Rockville, MD*

"I really recommend *My Many Colored Days* by Dr. Seuss. It teaches kids about emotions and that they're all okay to have, and it uses colors to describe them. It's Sam's favorite book."
—*Beth Miller, Novato, CA*

"My son liked the Touch and Feel books—the ones where you touch the soft bunny fur and the velvet horse. When he was a toddler, he loved the lift-the-flap books by Fisher-Price. He was always eager to see that there was something behind the flap."
—*Anita Good, Hewitt, NJ*

"*Brown Bear, Brown Bear, What Do You See?* and *Goodnight Moon* have been my favorites for all three of my daughters. I like the rhyming with Brown Bear—my kids pick up on that real fast—and I always read *Goodnight Moon* before bed."
—*Elicia Moore, Monrovia, CA*

"I love the Sandra Boynton books because their humor appeals to adults as well as to little ones. *Barnyard Dance* and *Hippos Go Berserk* are great ones."
—*Jessica Stygles, Toledo, OH*

Music

When buying music for little ones, try to look for something you won't mind hearing yourself again and again, because once babies take a liking to something, they often want to hear it over and over again.

THE THREE MUSICAL ARTISTS/RECORDINGS EVERY BABY SHOULD OWN

1. The Baby Einstein series, including *Baby Mozart, Baby Beethoven, Baby Bach, Baby Vivaldi,* and so on.
2. The Wiggles
3. Raffi

"Raffi has been a favorite since my thirteen-year-old was little. He's fun and silly, and the kids love him."
—*Missi Darnell, Acton, CA*

"We like classical orchestral music for babies. The Baby Einstein Company has some CDs that are great for babies and kids with classical tunes."
—*Kel Bright, Charleston, SC*

"*Baby Mozart* is great, as it stimulates their minds without being intrusive."
—*Rachel Hampton-Saint, Kent, England*

"We are Wiggles fanatics! They have taught my son so much. He loves music and loves singing their songs."
—*Anna Maria Johnson, Shreveport, LA*

"I like Raffi for toddlers, because his songs teach them about the earth and things around them. I also like classical versions of children's songs. I like the Baby Einstein series, mostly because the music is easy on everyone's ears."
—*Shelly Knight, Longmont, CO*

"I like the *Baby Mozart* songs and videos. Babies and toddlers are amazed with the bright colors and soft music, plus fun and silly images."
—*Eva Lindsey, Dallas, TX*

Television/Videos

We know that babies and toddlers don't need to watch any television. But we're also realistic. Sometimes we need fifteen minutes of uninterrupted time to get dinner on the table. When we do make the choice to allow our little ones to watch, though, we want to make sure that what they're watching is as beneficial to them as possible. We look for shows/videos that are educational and entertaining at the same time.

**OUR FIVE FAVORITE
TELEVISION SHOWS/VIDEOS FOR LITTLE ONES**

1. *Sesame Street*
2. Baby Einstein videos
3. *Blue's Clues*
4. *The Wiggles*
5. *Dora the Explorer*

"We started buying *Sesame Street* tapes when Avery was young, and she fell in love with Elmo instantly. The tapes aren't so annoying that the parent can't watch, and we are constantly amazed at the things she learns from these educational videos. We limit the television time, as we also want her to explore other activities, but she constantly asks when she'll get to watch Elmo!"
—*Billie Smith, Turpin, OK*

"*Blue's Clues* is educational and entertaining. I think it teaches children excellent problem-solving skills."
—*Kristen Math, Sartell, MN*

"I recommend *Dora the Explorer* and *The Wiggles*. The songs and colors are great for keeping children's attention."
—*Tanya Rosario, Bronx, NY*

"The Baby Einstein series really does seem to hold the interest of babies and kids. As they get older, the one with animals is a lot of fun."
—*Jennifer Rose, Ashland, MA*

"*Blue's Clues* and *Dora the Explorer* are two of my kids' favorites. I like the way both shows encourage the kids to remember three clues to solve the puzzle or the three landmarks they must pass to get where they are going."
—*Danielle Marion-Doyle, Donaldsonville, LA*

"I love *The Wiggles*. On rainy days, the girls really jump around to them, and I like the music. I resisted the urge to buy the tape for a long time, since they were the 'rage,' but I finally caved, and I am glad I did!"
—*Patricia Arnold, Westford, MA*

"My favorite TV show, by far, is *Sesame Street*. It's fun, educational, and entertaining for both my toddler and me."
—*Hannah Johnson, M.D., Elmhurst, IL*

"I recommend *Dora the Explorer* and *Blue's Clues*. Why? Because they are educational and also entertaining for the child."
—*Dafni Mauchley, Phelan, CA*

CHAPTER THIRTEEN

Sickness and Health

If you're lucky, the only health-related issue you'll face the first year is teething. More likely, you'll have at least one cold or ear infection, though. Don't fret. We're here with our best tips and tricks to get through it.

Teething

It's not exactly an illness, but it might as well be for some babies. Not only do they drool like crazy and chew on anything and everything in sight, but they can become cranky, feverish, restless (read: up all night), and even develop cold symptoms. Here are our best strategies for coping.

THE SEVEN BEST WAYS TO RELIEVE TEETHING PAIN

1. Teething rings
2. Cold or frozen washcloth
3. Tylenol or Motrin
4. Hyland's Teething Tablets
5. Frozen bagels or waffles to chew on
6. Popsicles
7. Baby Safe Feeder

"The very best method that I've used is to take a thin baby wash-cloth and knot one end. Wet the cloth, put it in a Ziploc bag, and freeze it. Let the baby chew on the frozen cloth (let thaw a bit if it's too cold for baby's hands). This numbs the gums and re-lives the itching and pressure of emerging teeth."
—*Stephanie Martin, Macomb, MI*

"I found ice pops work great for my kids. They love the way they taste, and they help numb their gums at the same time. There is also a thing you can get at the store called a Baby Safe Feeder that can hold fruit and ice cubes and things they would not normally be able to eat. With this, they can chew on these foods, but can't choke on them. It has a handle so they can hold it themselves. My son seemed to go through them pretty quickly, but I thought they were well worth it."
—*Brooke Ulinski, Levittown, PA*

"We used acetaminophen during the day to take the edge off, then ibuprofen at night as it lasts six to eight hours and eases the gum-swelling. We also had a special teether that vibrated when the child bit down on it. I don't know why it worked, but it did. Another teether that worked well was one that was filled with liq-uid and was freezable. I could see the relief on my daughter's face when she bit down on it."
—*Julie Bartlett, Bettendorf, IA*

"Hyland's Teething Tablets are amazing. I wish I had known about them with my oldest son."
—*Denine Scallen, Sammamish, WA*

"Frozen waffles work well; they have built-in spit cups!"
—*Lamiel Oesterreicher, Brooklyn, NY*

"Hyland's Teething Tablets and Hyland's Teething Gel work very well. I have found they seem to work better than Baby Orajel [R]. Also, a cold, wet, baby washcloth given to a baby to suck/teethe on seems to help."
—*Diane Bedrosian, M.D., Carlsbad, CA*

"My sons loved chewing on a frozen bagel when they were trying to cut teeth. It was sort of soft and tasted a lot better than a plastic ring."
—*Lori Stussie, Lawrence, KS*

"I discovered the Baby Safe Feeder after trying everything else first. I just put cut-up apple, pear, cantaloupe, whatever, in there, and he just bites away. It is a big drool-yielder, but well worth it, as I know it provided the best relief out of anything else we tried."
—*Beth Miller, Novato, CA*

When They Get Sick

Nothing is more heartbreaking than seeing your innocent babe get sick. They can't sleep; they can't eat; they just lose all of their spunk. Fortunately, first babies usually get sick less frequently than subsequent children, and by the time you have your second (or third, fourth, fifth . . .), you'll have been through it all. Here are our best ideas for coping when baby isn't feeling quite up to snuff.

Taking Baby's Temperature

In general, we like using the ear thermometer for quick readings. It's fast, noninvasive, and if you know how to use an ear thermometer well, we've found it's great. Unfortunately, we're not all experts at using it, which means readings can vary widely, depending on the angle at which you insert the thermometer into the child's ear and how long you keep it there.

Other alternatives for quick readings include under-the-arm strips, strips across the forehead, and the pacifier thermometer.

We are big fans of the new digital thermometers for rectal or axillary (under the arm) temperatures. These are not like the older digital thermometers. They are super fast, registering readings in seconds.

OUR FAVORITE METHOD

Axillary (under the arm)

"I prefer to take my daughter's temperature under her arm. This way, I can get the temperature I need to get, and I can comfort her at the same time."
—*Jessica Gane, Brookhaven, PA*

"I like to take Joseph's temperature under his arm while I'm nursing him. He stays very still because he's concentrating on nursing instead of what I'm doing."
—*Sara Hammontree, Mountain Home, AR*

"I would have to say I like the new Vicks underarm sticker wearable/disposable thermometer. It sticks to the baby's underarm and can be read all day long. The ear thermometers don't seem to give an accurate reading because the ear canal is too narrow to accommodate the part of the thermometer that goes into the ear. With the underarm thermometer, if I suspect my daughter has a temperature, I can stick one on and leave it there, and read it multiple times throughout the day, so I can see if the medicine is bringing the temperature down."
—*Karen Hurst, Roseville, CA*

When Baby Has a Cold

Most doctors don't recommend giving very young babies cold medicines, largely because they don't work on young children. That means you have to resort to mom-tested comfort strategies. Here are our favorites.

OUR FIVE FAVORITE COLD REMEDIES

1. Sit in a steamy shower.
2. Give baby a warm bath with a children's vapor bath product or a rubdown with a children's vapor cream.
3. Give baby plenty of rest, fluids, and your tender loving care.

4. Use saline nasal drops.

5. Use a vaporizer.

"Turning the shower on hot and sitting in the bathroom lets the steam relieve congestion. Menthol baby baths and a cool mist humidifier also do the trick."
—*Becky Gaston, Owensboro, KY*

"I like bringing the baby into a steamy bathroom after taking a hot shower. I get the relaxation of the shower, and she gets the nasal clearance that only steam seems to accomplish. It helps if I allow the water to continually run after bringing her in there. All natural and no adverse effects."
—*Caren Sadikman, M.D., Rochester, MN*

"I use homemade nasal drops: one-fourth teaspoon of salt plus eight ounces of boiled water, cooled completely."
—*Sabrina Lane, Boise, ID*

"I recommend rest (to let the body heal), fluids to rehydrate the body, and lots of love (who doesn't like that anytime)?"
—*Holly Cocchiola, Bethlehem, CT*

"I usually just take my son into the bathroom with me while a steaming hot shower runs to help him sleep better with a cold. It clears him up a bit and makes it easier to wipe or suction his nose with a bulb syringe after ten minutes or so in the 'steam room.' I've never given him any medication for a cold, as my pediatrician advises against it."
—*Beth Miller, Novato, CA*

OUR FAVORITE PAIN-RELIEVER/FEVER-REDUCER

Tylenol

"I like Tylenol because it works quickly and my kids always liked the taste."
—*Donnica L. Moore, M.D., Branchburg, NJ*

"Tylenol, Tylenol, Tylenol. It doesn't interfere with other medications, and it doesn't have any side effects. I feel safe using it, which is very important to a new mom!"

—Staci Paro, Lynn, MA

Getting Them to Take Medicine

With all the fun flavors medicine comes in nowadays (grape, cherry, bubble gum, etc.), you'd think babies would love taking it. After all, it has to taste better than rice cereal, right? But some babies are tough customers when it comes to taking any kind of medicine, no matter how good it's supposed to taste. Try these ideas when your little one is fighting you every step of the way.

THREE SURE-FIRE WAYS TO GET A SQUIRMY BABY TO TAKE MEDICINE

1. Squirt it into the baby's cheek.
2. Mix it with something they like.
3. Make it fun.

"In the Emergency Room, we have tried them all. I tend to give them something they like, then give them the medicine with the same voice (mmm . . . cherries). Otherwise, crush the pill form into applesauce or pudding (butterscotch actually works best) and make it seem like a treat because they are sick. For really young babies, shoot it toward the back of the mouth with a syringe a little at a time and chase it with something they like to drink."

—Michelle Gebhard, D.O., White Plains, NY

"I always put them in their seat or in the high chair, reclined, but not lying down, and I squirt some in the back corner of the cheek and put their pacifier in their mouth right away. So even if the medicine is really yucky, if they have an attachment to the pacifier, they are going to suck on it, and presto, the medicine is down before they know what happened."

—Brooke Kuhns, Dayton, OH

TO CONTRIBUTE TO THE NEXT EDITION, VISIT WWW.GALLAGHERGUIDE.COM

"I would put it in a dropper and squeeze the medicine down the side of the baby's mouth (along the inside of the cheek) and then blow into the baby's face to make her swallow (just a little puff, like you're blowing out a birthday candle). A pharmacist recommended putting the medicine in grape juice or chocolate milk. He explained that these two substances will mask most bad-tasting medicines. I tried this a couple of times, but you have to be careful to make sure the baby drinks all of it. Also, always check with a pharmacist before mixing medicine with anything."
—*Julie Bartlett, Bettendorf, IA*

"We make a big deal out of it in our house. When it's time to take it for the first time, we make it seem exciting, almost like she is getting an extra special treat. We treat it like she is getting an extended dessert. I swear the last time she was on amoxicillin, she got excited every time she saw the medicine bottle. We've never had a difficult time with her taking medicine."
—*Donna Davidson, Weymouth, MA*

Getting a Good Night's Rest When They Are Sick

Nighttime is the worst time for little ones when they're sick. Illnesses seem to get worse at night, and it's hard to sleep when you're all stuffed up. Here's what we do to help them sleep at night and feel better overall.

THE FIVE BEST WAYS TO HELP A SICK BABY SLEEP

1. Give lots of tender loving care.
2. Use a soothing children's vapor lotion or vapor bath product.
3. Elevate the baby's head.
4. Sleep with baby or let him fall asleep on you.
5. Use a vaporizer.

"Letting small ones sleep in a car seat or carrier lets them breathe better."
—*Veronica Wilson, Chattanooga, TN*

"Roll up a towel and put it under his mattress at the head of the bed to help relieve nasal congestion."
—*Katie Conroy, Palos Hills, IL*

"I would rock my children to sleep or let them lie down with me in my bed when they were sick or couldn't sleep. I also would sometimes give them a little massage with some oil."
—*Brenda Dintiman, M.D., Fairfax, VA*

"Cosleeping is a lifesaver when little ones are sick. Nothing is more comforting than to cuddle up with Mommy or Daddy when they are not feeling well. This has the added benefit of being right there if they get sicker during the night."
—*Megan Miles, Marysville, WA*

"I give them a nice warm bath, then nurse until they fall asleep. When my babies were little, I slept with them in the rocker to help keep their heads elevated, so they didn't choke. Also, I could feel if a fever broke out."
—*Barbara Nichols, Okeechobee, FL*

"The humidifier has been a great help with this. Not only does the moisture help, but it has a sound that lulls them to sleep."
—*Wendy Douglas, Margate, FL*

Brushing Teeth

We believe that earlier is better when it comes to teaching proper dental hygiene. Even if your baby has only one or two teeth, you can begin practicing brushing. When your child is older, squirmier, and potentially more defiant, here are our favorite tricks.

FIVE CLEVER WAYS TO MAKE BRUSHING TEETH EASY AND FUN

1. Brush together.
2. Give them fun toothbrushes.
3. Buy toothpaste that tastes good.
4. Make it part of your daily routine.
5. Sing a toothbrushing song.

"Liam is a copycat, so we get him to brush his teeth by sitting him on the counter while we brush our teeth. He loves to do anything we do. We do have to help him make sure he gets them all brushed well, but he doesn't seem to mind since he's participating in the same activity we are."
—Heather French, Fishers, IN

"I get them cool toothbrushes. My boys have Spiderman and Bob the Builder toothbrushes and Buzz Lightyear toothpaste, so they do it without my even having to ask."
—Brooke Ulinski, Levittown, PA

"I play the zoo game with my kids. I tell them I can see alligators, elephants, and zebras in their mouths, and then we try to brush them away. This has always gotten a huge giggle out of them, and they let me spend more time brushing each tooth."
—Stephanie Smith, Alexandria, KY

"We have our daughter brush hers when we brush ours. We play a game and sing a song, 'This is the way we brush our teeth, brush our teeth, this is the way we brush our teeth so we can get them clean.' My daughter loves it."
—Debby Madrid, Elkhart, IN

CHAPTER FOURTEEN

MAKING AND PRESERVING MEMORIES

You wouldn't exactly take a baby or toddler to an amusement park for fun, but there are things you can do together that are enjoyable for both of you. Here are our favorites.

Fifteen Fabulous Ways to Have Fun with Your Little One

1. Take a walk . . . around the neighborhood, to a park, or a playground.
2. Sing to them and dance with them.
3. Take a Mommy and Me, Gymboree, or baby music class.
4. Give your baby a massage.
5. Go to the supermarket.
6. Go to a coffeeshop.
7. Join a playgroup.
8. Visit a farmers' market.
9. Go swimming.
10. Feed the ducks.
11. Enjoy free events at bookstores, libraries, craft stores, etc.

12. Go to the zoo.

13. Take a bath together.

14. Go to special movies for moms (shown at select times) with your baby.

15. Visit the grandparents.

"I loved taking my son in his sling to the local farmers' market. He loved seeing all the people, and I enjoyed getting out and looking at the flowers and produce. Once he was old enough to eat solids, I would give him sample slices of peaches, nectarines, and plums to gum at. He still loves eating fresh fruit."
—*Rachel Hulan, Lake Forest, CA*

"I go for stroller walks in beautiful places. I've gone to Nordstrom for first outings because they have a nursing lounge in the ladies' room. I've gone with groups of new moms to middle-of-the-week movie matinees and then empty fancy restaurants for lunch. There's a movie theater where I live that, one night a week, reserves itself for parents with babies under a year old. I have a standing lunch date with a friend, and every week, after my mothers' group, the baby and I meet her for lunch. I also take postpartum exercise classes where child care is provided."
—*Stacey Sklar, Oakland, CA*

"We did a Moms and Babies class at our hospital until Bella was four months old. It was good for us to bond with each other, as well as with other moms and babies. We also did an infant massage class. Now, after each bath, I give Bella a massage with her baby lotion. She loves it. We also did a playgroup with other new moms and babies until I started work when Bella was ten months old."
—*Kris Rivas, Denver, CO*

"I think baby massage is great for both babies and new moms. Take a class or read a book before your baby arrives, so you know what to do. Put on some lullabies, (which soothe new parents as much as they do new babies!), break out the apricot seed oil, and gently rub your baby all over."
—*Amelia Stinson-Wesley, Morganton, NC*

"Just getting outdoors is a wonderful way to spend time with the baby. I would take my son in his stroller around the neighborhood twice a day for half-hour walks and point out all the birds, trees, animals, cars, and trucks. It was a nice way for us both to get out of the house, while I was getting the exercise I needed."
—Lisa McDonald, Maitland, FL

"The park is an amazing place, especially for a little one. Putting my daughter on a swing for the first time will forever be etched into my memory. The look of sheer delight on her face was precious."
—Megan Martin, Crystal Lake, IL

"Swimming is a fun, fantastic outing. It's good exercise for the mom, and babies, if introduced early, will love the feeling."
—Barbara Nichols, Okeechobee, FL

"I found that I was always looking for things to do in the early morning to get my mind off of how desperately tired I was. My first was a very early riser and demanded entertainment first thing in the morning. At that hour, I was just not capable of a perky game of peekaboo! So instead, I went to early morning places (where I always found other mothers, by the way)—farmer's markets, Sunday brunch at the Marriott, the 24-hour Home Depot, coffee shops, etc. At that age, a baby doesn't care where you are, they just want to see people and go places. I would plop her in the Baby Björn and just walk, and sometimes knock off an errand to boot. Then we would head home by 10 a.m. to crash for a nap."
—Diana Molavi, M.D., Baltimore, MD

"As babies grow, story time at the local library or bookstore is always a hit. I took my babies to plays, children's book theme characters' appearances, and sing-a-longs—all for free. Look in your local paper for entertainment in your area. You can also find that information on the Internet. AOL has a local guide section on their main screen. I use it all the time."
—Dawn Kirnon, M.D., New York, NY

"With my first, I had a really good time meeting my mom—his grandmother—for at least a weekly lunch. This got us all out and together from an early age and made it easier to meet, since we lived about an hour apart at the time. Grandma was always happy to hold the baby if need be, so I got to enjoy lunch, and Grandma was able to forge a special bond with her grandson, too."
—Janette Gilman, Potomac, MD

Birthday Parties

There is only one hard and fast rule about planning kids' birthday parties: They should be designed so the birthday kid has fun. While this may seem like an obvious concept, it doesn't always work out that way. Sometimes the reasons are obligatory: The parents feel obligated to invite fifty people so that dad's second cousin, twice removed, won't feel left out. Other times, they're responding to peer pressure: Everyone else in the neighborhood throws huge galas for their kids' birthdays, so the parents feel obligated to do the same. Still other times, it's a matter of returning social favors: The parents and child have gotten invited to so many friends' kids' parties, they feel obligated to return the favor.

Whatever the reason, kids' birthday parties have gotten bigger and more elaborate (and stressful) than ever before in recent years. Here's how to keep the party fun for everyone involved.

EIGHT GREAT SECRETS
FOR BIRTHDAY PARTY SUCCESS
1. Make sure it is age-appropriate.
2. Make it easy on yourself.
3. Limit the number of guests.
4. Do it at home.
5. Keep it simple.
6. Give it a theme.
7. Have a game plan.
8. Do it outside.

"I have learned that I do not have to go all out or compete with my children's friends when planning parties. Just as long as the focus is on my birthday child, we all have a good day."
—*Keli Loveland, Bartlett, TN*

"When my daughter turned one, I didn't want to go all out because I knew she would get overstimulated and wouldn't remember it anyway. We had a small Winnie the Pooh party with close relatives. I have to say it was the best party I have ever seen."
—*Becky Gaston, Owensboro, KY*

"The best party I have thrown was a bowling party. It was not a lot of money. They set up, played games with the kids, gave us our own room for lunch, cake, and gifts, and they cleaned up!"
—*Elicia Moore, Monrovia, CA*

"When my children (now in their thirties) were growing up, we just had our friends and their children over to the house, put up balloons, and served coffee, birthday cake, and ice cream. Basically, I think it's the people who make the party, not the fancy place where everyone tries to outdo each other."
—*Linda Linguvic, New York, NY*

"That rule you always hear (and that I always ignored) about the number of guests being the kid's age plus one should be a mantra for all mothers!"
—*Donnica L. Moore, M.D., Branchburg, NJ*

"I am a preschool teacher and have helped lots of moms plan parties. Young children need some planned activities or they go crazy. Having a game plan for the party is a great idea. I once helped plan a Halloween birthday party. I made a timetable list for the mother to use. We planned the two hours, so that every ten to fifteen minutes, there was something new to do. With arriving, eating, and activities, the two hours flew by and there was no chaos. The kids had a great time, and the parents who stayed enjoyed it as well."
—*Susan Dobratz, Plymouth, MA*

"We had a monster birthday party. We had a 'monster stomp' activity where the kids stomped on balloons (monsters), 'Pin the Eye on the Monster' (Mike from Monsters, Inc.), and made monster puppets for the craft. The theme was orange and green, so we had orange and green balloons, streamers, napkins, and plates. I served orange and green Kool-Aid and had all snacks in orange and green cups."

—Denine Scallen, Sammamish, WA

"I would say the best was one that was at a picnic area on the outside of a playground. It was really nice for the kids to be able to go and play, then come back to the picnic area and eat after a cookout."

—Veronica Wilson, Chattanooga, TN

Preserving Memories

While we're going through it, the sleepless nights, poopy diapers, and teething pain may seem like they will never end. But the baby years go by in a flash, and if you don't record the memorable moments, you may forget them.

SEVEN SENSATIONAL WAYS TO PRESERVE MEMORIES FROM THE BABY YEARS

1. Baby book
2. Scrapbook
3. Keepsake box
4. Journal
5. Pictures
6. Calendar
7. Time capsule

"I like to use a baby book to store memories. Don't forget to add pictures of the kids' playgroup and neighborhood friends. These will be nice to look back on. One baby book I have had you paste a postage stamp from the time of your baby's birth. Adding

items like stamps, menus, and movie ticket stubs let the kids know what our lives were like when they were born."
—*Kim DelPrete, Gaithersburg, MD*

"I use a baby book, photos, and journaling. I am also having a quilt made of all my daughter's favorite newborn clothes. Each square will be from a different clothing item. It's a great way to remember her outfits without having to keep them all in a box, and a good way to display them, too!"
—*Kris Pena, M.D., Ventura, CA*

"I've been making an e-scrapbook with a desktop publishing program. It's easy to e-mail the files or send a disk to friends and family. And we are able to store backups in no space at all. If you save in html format, you can even add animated graphics."
—*Angel Smith, Brooksville, FL*

"I have two things. First is a box which contains some special items that I want to keep to show him when he's older, for example, a new diaper, which is tiny because he was a premature baby, and also the onesie he was wearing on the day he was taken to another hospital for emergency heart surgery. I also made a scrapbook, which contains photos, foot- and handprints, etc."
—*Katie Anne Gustafsson, Eskilstuna, Sweden*

"We have a memory box for each of our children. Things we put in there are newspapers from their birthdays, including the day they were born, special cards they receive, and any other items we want to cherish. I also keep a notebook, and whenever my kids say something cute or funny, I write it down along with the date."
—*Michelle Laney, Helena, AL*

"I like to have a keepsake box. Honestly, I tried to have a baby book, but I failed to write in it. It seems so restrictive and time-consuming. With a keepsake box, I can put in little mementos, like locks of hair, hospital bracelets, scraps of material, and I can go

through it whenever I want. I imagine myself pulling these things out in the future, telling great stories about each thing to my children."
—*Christina Stevens, Endicott, NY*

"I sew, so I kept all of my favorite/memorable outfits and made them into a baby memory quilt. I sewed the outfits onto a blanket that was special. When she gets into her 'big girl' bed, it will be her quilt. I think I will save it for her when she grows out of it and give it back to her on her wedding day.

"I also have a time box with newspapers and magazines from the day/month she was born. She will be able to look back and see what was going on when she was born."
—*Genevieve Molloy, Guttenberg, NJ*

"I started a journal to my daughter when I first found out I was pregnant. I don't write in it every day, but rather, once every couple of months or when she does something especially great (first words, first day she walked, first time she said, 'I love you'). I plan to continue writing in it as she grows up and then, either on her graduation day or her wedding day, I plan to give it to her as a gift.

"We also invested in a digital camera right before she was born, and we have taken over one thousand photos of her first two years. We have them all in a photo gallery on the web, so that our friends and family all over the country can keep up with her growth. I am currently printing the photos a few at a time and working on scrapbooks as well."
—*Heather Meininger, Charlotte, NC*

"My kids have baby books, time capsules and scrapbooks. But my favorite way is what we called [baby name]'s Special Tote. All it is is a Rubbermaid container (I prefer Rubbermaid, as they seal better) and inside we have a picture of the pregnancy test, the newspaper from the day they were born, special outfits (coming home from the hospital, baptism, first Christmas, etc.), crib bedding, baptism outfit, really anything special that you want to keep for them. Then I use the time capsule for letters to them and stuff that has happened in the world."
—*Ange Gregory, Stanwood, IA*

"I keep a calendar handy and jot notes into it daily. Then I can sit down and transfer all the cute things they do and say when I have time to get out the albums. Otherwise, I forget what happened by the time I am able to get out the major memento-savers!"

—*Denise Greenwood, M.D., Little Rock, AR*

"I kept a milestone calendar for the first two years of my daughter's life and plan to do so again for our son. It was much easier to put a sticker on the date to record a milestone than have to remember to drag out a big bulky book. I also loved the idea of having a picture every month. It was a great way to watch and see how she's grown. I tried to make sure that the picture either reflected the major milestone of the month, or represented what she was 'into' at the time. The calendar I had had a little pocket page for each month, and you could put keepsakes and notes in it."

—*Megan Martin, Crystal Lake, IL*

Pictures

Of course, you'll take tons of pictures of your sweet angel yourself in your own backyard (and at the park, in the high chair, in the bath, etc.), and now with digital cameras, it's easier than ever to make high-quality prints in a wide variety of sizes. But we don't all own digital cameras yet, and sometimes we just like the idea of getting professional pictures taken at a studio.

THE ABSOLUTE BEST PLACE
TO GET BABY PICTURES TAKEN

Sears Portrait Studios

"Sears does a good job and often has coupons. They let me change my daughter's outfits three times in one sitting, which I don't think other places allow. The SmileSavers club is a good

deal—you pay $30 one time, and no more sitting fees for two years (we've had four sittings by twenty-two months)."
—*Marlo Greenspan, Boyds, MD*

"We have been going to the same Sears studio and having the same photographer taking our kids' pictures since our daughter was a month old (she is now five). And the photographer is now taking our son's pictures. I love going to Sears because their backgrounds are wonderful—they just got new ones in, and they are sooo full of detail. I like being able to pick and choose the photos I want, I love being able to get the size I want and need, unlike most places. They have really nice 'extras,' like greeting cards, birth announcements, portrait creations (which let you make your photos personal by adding borders or making photos black and white or sepia toned), etc. They are always adding new things that make it really nice not to have to get the same old thing."
—*Ange Gregory, Stanwood, IA*

"I always get my pictures taken at Sears because they have great coupons and a baby club that allows you to skip sitting fees for two years."
—*Kari Lomanno, Chesapeake, VA*

"They always have great sales, and they have the SmileSavers plan. We have tried other places, but they are always too expensive, and the pictures don't come out the way we want them to."
—*Tara Betteridge, Fort Lewis, WA*

"Sears is the best, bar none! The photographers are always GREAT there. The waiting rooms cater to kids, and they have great specials. Truly, the photographers make all the difference in the world. A photographer who is only there for the paycheck will just snap the shots, but one who coaxes personality onto film will make your portraits priceless!"
—*Angel Smith, Brooksville, FL*

CHAPTER FIFTEEN

TODDLERS

Peer pressure is the enemy of all toddler mommies. If it weren't for our friends, neighbors, relatives, and even acquaintances on the street, most of us couldn't care less whether our toddlers or preschoolers still used a bottle or pacifier, whether they slept in a crib or bed, or how soon they were potty trained.

But once our babes get to be about two, the Mommy Police seem to swoop down in full force, scrutinizing our little ones for any lingering signs of babyhood and criticizing us if they appear. It's as if our toddlers are supposed to become fully functioning members of society at the ripe old age of two!

The important thing to remember is that all this "expert advice" and "tsk-tsking" is all a bunch of bunk. You don't go to back-to-school nights at elementary school and hear parents talking about trying to get their third-graders potty trained or their kindergarteners off the bottle. So relax. Everything will fall into place exactly when it's supposed to.

And the next time you encounter the Mommy Police, just nod and smile, the same as you did when the competitive mommies you know bragged that they went through thirty-six hours of labor without an epidural or their babies slept through the night at six weeks old.

Sure, it happens. But you've read this book, and you know the real truth: We all struggle through this crazy wonderful experience called motherhood. And no one gets through it without a challenge or two.

In fact, we firmly believe that the universe divvies up mommy tortures equally, so if you had trouble with colic and poor sleeping habits the first year, you'll probably sail through toddlerhood. On the other hand, your friend with the epidural-free labor and the baby who slept through the night at six weeks could struggle with potty training for years. We're not trying to wish difficulties on your friends, but hey, it might make you feel better!

Our Five Best Ideas for Getting Rid of the Pacifier

1. Wean off the pacifier as early as possible.
2. Restrict it to nap time and nighttime only.
3. Go cold turkey and grit your teeth.
4. Cut the tips off and tell him the pacifiers are broken.
5. Have your child give it to the bunnies, Santa Claus, or the pacifier fairy in exchange for a toy.
6. Do it when she's ready.

"I am firm believer that you have to go cold turkey. I had no choice when my daughter was about eighteen months old. She was biting the nipples off, and it was becoming a real choking hazard. This kid was addicted, too. She always had a binky for nap and bedtime and whenever else she was fussy. We got rid of all the binkies in one fell swoop, told her they were 'broken,' cut the nipples off and even let her try that one once or twice. She fussed a lot for the first few days, but within a week, she did not miss it."
—Dana Baedke, Chalfont, PA

"The binky fairy! When the child is older (aged two or three), they can put all their binkies into a brown lunch bag and leave it

for the binky fairy. The binky fairy takes the binkies while they're asleep and leaves a 'big kid' cuddle toy as a replacement. A nice, cuddly teddy bear is one suggestion, especially since toddlers usually rely on their binkies to get to sleep."
—*Jennifer Young, Bethesda, MD*

"My son was two-and-a-half by the time we were able to get rid of the pacifier. After trying several other ideas, the one that finally worked for us was cutting a small slit in the pacifier, so it didn't work correctly, and giving it back to him. He put it in his mouth and when he tried to suck on it, it didn't feel the same, so he gave it back to us and told us it was broken.

"We told him that we couldn't fix it and that maybe he should put it in the trash. He put it in the trash in the living room (it was empty except for the paci), and didn't ask for it again until that night. Then he went and got it out of the trash and brought it to us. We washed it and gave it back to him, he sucked on it, said it was broken, took it out of his mouth and slept holding it that night and the next. Then he left it on his nightstand for a few days and finally, we just tossed it. He never really asked for it or looked for it after that."
—*Heather French, Fishers, IN*

"Do it on the child's time schedule, not your own. One day, my daughter just decided she didn't need hers anymore. Another trick is to have the pacifier fairy pick it up and leave a new toy/doll/truck."
—*Angel Broussard, Lake Charles, LA*

"When my son was ready to give up the pacifier, we told him we needed to send it to the 'Pacifier Depot,' a place which collected pacifiers from big kids and redistributed them to babies who needed them. We wrapped his beloved pacifier in a little box and addressed and stamped it. My son put the box in our mailbox for the mailman (my husband intercepted). We then went to the store to pick out a 'big kid' gift for him.

NOTE: First make sure that your child has a stuffed animal or other lovey that can meet his needs for comfort. The first night or two may be a bit teary, as the child realizes the pacifier is gone forever. You can comfort the child and reinforce the fact that the lovey is there for him, too."

—*Sidney Marks, Menlo Park, CA*

"Keep them out of the house, so you can't give in and start using them again."

—*Robyn Greenhouse, Gaithersburg, MD*

Three Strategies for Stopping Thumb-Sucking

1. Use rewards.
2. Offer an alternative, such as holding a doll.
3. Ignore it, and let the child do it on his own time, even if it takes until college!

"Thumb-sucking is tough because the thumb is attached to your child. It's not like you can take it away (though I'd like to some days). I have two thumb-suckers, and I've found that if I ignore the habit, they suck their thumbs less often than if I constantly remind them to 'take the thumb out.' I don't allow my children to talk to me with the thumb in their mouths. I also find that they'll suck more if they are bored or watching TV, so I will find something to engage them, like a good book or art project. I feel that unless the habit is causing severe problems with their speech or teeth, you should not push your child to stop. Let them work it out on their own."

—*Stephanie Martin, Macomb, MI*

"Use positive reinforcement—stickers for every day/hour/afternoon, etc. that he/she goes without sucking. Replace thumb-sucking with a more healthy/acceptable alternative stress-reliever, such as holding a doll, straw, or other small object that can be kept in a pocket and pulled out in times of stress."

—*Kris Pena, M.D., Ventura, CA*

"I sucked my thumb until I was eighteen. Never had a problem. Your peers prevent you from doing it too much for fear of looking silly."
—*Rachel Hampton-Saint, Kent, England*

"I think children must outgrow this on their own. My kindergartener did not suck his thumb in school. Children are aware; they just need to want to do it, too."
—*Lori Burgess, Bingham, ME*

Three Ways to Make an Easy Leap from the Crib to a Bed

1. Get the child involved in the process by letting her pick out the bed or bedding, or help you move stuffed animals to the new bed.
2. Put the bed in the room with the crib for a period of time and allow him to take naps in it or just look at it.
3. Make a big fuss about how fun it will be or how cute the new sheets are, etc.

"I put the bed in his room for a week or so before I actually had him sleep in it at all. Then we started with just naps. After that, he actually asked to sleep in it and said the crib was for babies."
—*Brooke Kuhns, Dayton, OH*

"We bought her a little toddler bed and made a big fuss about her 'princess bed' and she couldn't wait to sleep in it."
—*Kate Steiman, Toms River, NJ*

"We waited until he was receptive. We would visit the bed departments at stores and think about it, but I waited until he wanted a big bed. Generally, waiting until a child initiates a major change (whenever possible) or at least guiding the idea for a while so that they feel some involvement in the decision is helpful. Allowing them to choose sheets is helpful, too."
—*Sarah Pletcher, East Lansing, MI*

"Involve your child in the process. Talk about how much she has grown and mention the things she can do now that she could not do when she was a baby. Use this as a base for introducing the idea of moving to a new bed. Let your child move her favorite blanket or stuffed animal and help you set up the new bed."
—Elicia Moore, Monrovia, CA

"My kids are close in age. My oldest son was eighteen months old when he gave up his crib to let his baby brother sleep in the crib. He did it on his own. He was thrilled to sleep in his bed with Mickey Mouse sheets and blankets."
—Connie Choate, Gardner, KS

The Quick and Easy Way to Potty Training

The first step in potty training is to look for signs of readiness. Here are the cues we noticed:

1. Waking up from naps dry and staying dry all night long.
2. Talking about the potty, asking about it, wanting to learn about it.
3. Showing interest when you or other family members go to the bathroom.
4. Wanting to sit on the potty, either with or without a diaper and/or clothes on.
5. Telling you when they are about to have a bowel movement (this sensation is usually felt first).
6. Asking you to change his diaper.
7. Reporting that other children are using the potty at day care or preschool and being interested in it.
8. Being able to physically pull her pants up and down.
9. Pulling at his diapers or hiding (e.g., going behind furniture) to have a bowel movement.

But remember, some children may be physically ready and may even show signs of interest, but are still not yet fully emotionally ready. If your child exhibits positive signs and you want to test the waters, go for it. But try not to put too much pressure on your child or react to peer pressure yourself.

With potty training, one sure-fire rule applies: You can NEVER wait too long. As long as you show the child the potty, tell her what it is for (e.g., "This is where you put your pee-pee and poo-poo when you're ready to go"), you've done all you need to do. Your child can figure out the rest for himself.

OUR SIX BIGGEST MISTAKES AND MOST IMPORTANT LESSONS WE LEARNED FROM POTTY TRAINING

1. Let the child—not you—be in control.
2. Be patient when he has accidents or she has to go to the bathroom five times in an hour.
3. Let her choose where she wants to go, whether she wants to use a child-sized potty chair, an insert on the big potty, or just the big potty by itself.
4. Rewards and bribes can work, but they can also backfire. Tread lightly, and use sparingly.
5. If the challenge is physical (i.e., he can't feel when he's wet), use training pants or cloth underwear instead of Pull-Ups.
6. Accept accidents without comment. Carry a change of clothes (or two or three) with you when you go out.

"I learned that you cannot force the issue. Children will master the potty when they, not you, are ready. If you have started training and your child is having several accidents a day, they aren't ready yet. Back off and return to training in a week or two."
—Stephanie Martin, Macomb, MI

"I learned that charts, stickers, and rewards don't always work. Sometimes just giving the kids time to mature makes potty training easier. When my second was ready, even though it was about a year later than the first, he was ready. By giving my second one

time to grow and allowing him to be ready, it made the transition so much easier."
—*Robyn Greenhouse, Gaithersburg, MD*

"With my first son, I knew he knew what the potty was for, as he had used it a handful of times. Then he just refused to use it. He was quickly approaching three years old, and I was getting frustrated. He started having a fit anytime I would even mention using the potty. Finally, one day I just gave him all the power. I told him that he could wear diapers as long as he wanted, and I would not mention the potty anymore. I told him that he was a big boy now and was big enough to decide when to use the potty.

"Later that day, he went in his diaper and started crying for me not to be mad at him. I never punished him for not using the potty, so I knew this was a test to see if I really meant what I said. In my most sincere voice, I assured him that I was happy to change his diapers as long as he chose to wear them. The very next day, he started using the potty and never regressed.

"Learning from the experience with my first son, I decided NOT to potty train my second son. I put the potty chair in the bathroom and explained what it was for and would occasionally ask him if he would like to use it and took his lead 100 percent. He trained himself by thirty-three months, and there was no stress or frustration involved at all.

"My best advice is to let the kids decide when they are ready. They know you can't MAKE them do it, and if you make it a power struggle, they will win."
—*Sherry Rennie, Rialto, CA*

"I learned to carry a lot of clothes (for changing) with me when going out."
—*Alejandra Dozal, El Paso, TX*

"Pull-Ups, in some ways, work against toilet training, once they reach a certain stage. Go back to the old-fashioned way of using cloth underwear with vinyl underwear over it."
—*Deshawn Anderson-Drew, Apopka, FL*

TO CONTRIBUTE TO THE NEXT EDITION, VISIT WWW.GALLAGHERGUIDE.COM

"Don't force it. When the child is truly ready, it is easy and quick with few accidents. The moms I know who started really working it at the first slightest sign of interest had so much more of a struggle, and the 'training' process was fairly prolonged. They had lots of accidents, had to bribe the child, or had to work their schedules around potty training.

"I was too lazy to go through all that trouble and didn't want to spend hours in the bathroom. I preferred to keep my daughter in diapers as long as possible, because I found it was easier for me. What is worse than a child in training needing to go when you are in public without access to a good, clean restroom?

"Some kids are more motivated to get out of diapers than others. Mine didn't care that much, so I didn't make a big deal about it. It was so much easier for both of us. When other moms bragged about their children being potty trained at eighteen months, I just said we weren't ready. And I was glad because I didn't have to worry about public restrooms or working my schedule around the daily poop."
—*Jamie Hunley, San Diego, CA*

"The biggest struggle for me is just having patience with my daughter during potty training—being willing to go to the potty four or five times during a restaurant meal, sitting in a public restroom for ten to fifteen minutes waiting for a poopy, not getting upset when she has an accident as we're running late out the door, etc. As we are still going through these stages, I am realizing how important it is to not rush her or become upset, knowing that psychologically, this is a sensitive subject."
—*Kris Pena, M.D., Ventura, CA*

"The three biggest lessons we learned were that Pull-Ups are a no-no, diapers can be a lot easier than potty training, and that it did no good to start early. My son trained late, but never ever had an accident. My daughter showed early interest, we moved on it, and then had accidents for the next several years."
—*Janette Gilman, Potomac, MD*

"Just because a child is old enough to understand the concept and reasons behind potty training, does not mean that they are willing to learn. By waiting until my daughter was older than the average age for training, it took her less than a day to get trained."

—*Brandi Leach, Fort Worth, TX*

Monsters, Clowns, Costumed Characters, and Other Scary Stuff

It's often surprising to first-time parents that toddlers and preschoolers are afraid of seemingly fun things, like clowns or Santa Claus, long before they are afraid of monsters and other typical scary stuff. Regardless of what the fear is, here are our best ideas for coping with it.

1. Let him know it's okay to be scared; don't force him to interact with the clown or character.
2. Spray the air around her bed with pretend "monster repellant" or real air freshener to ward off nighttime fears—or give her a water bottle to spray herself.
3. Blow kisses to the monsters.
4. Let her use a nightlight or other light.
5. Show him monsters can be friendly by watching *Monsters, Inc.* or *Sesame Street*.
6. Give your child her own personal superhero.

"Disney's *Monsters, Inc.* is a fabulous film that takes the scare out of the idea of the monster under the bed. Our daughter had a brief period of being terribly afraid of the dark, but once she met Sully, she now carries him into any dark room without fear! He is her hero!"

—*Chaya Reich, Los Angeles, CA*

"I had one child that was terribly afraid of clowns from the ages of two to four. He would melt into tears every time he saw one. For a while, I avoided things like the circus because he just couldn't handle it. When he was around four, I took him to see a man who plays a local clown in my area. I let him meet the man without makeup and then, he was allowed to watch him put his makeup on. I think realizing that there was a real person under the bright makeup and big clothes helped my son conquer his fear.

"Same thing with monsters and the dark. Let your child look under the bed with the lights on and then turn them off and give him a flashlight to see for himself that there isn't anything there. Sometimes the fear is really of the unknown rather than of the monster, the dark, or clowns."
—*Stephanie Martin, Macomb, MI*

"When she comes running out screaming, 'It's a monster!' we ask her if it's Cookie Monster or Elmo. It really works!"
—*Genevieve Molloy, Guttenberg, NJ*

"I just recently had a situation with a lot of nightmares and monsters in the room. I now spray air freshener in the twins' room before they go to sleep. They want to watch me spray it. And they know the monsters do not like this smell, so they won't come to their room. They even remind me to spray if I have forgotten. And unlike spraying water or pretending to spray, they smell it, so they know it's working."
—*Andrea Suissa, Olney, MD*

"This is just beginning at our house. But so far, blowing kisses to the imaginary offenders works."
—*Cara Vincens, Thionville, France*

"I gave my kids a small squirt bottle with water in it as 'monster spray.' They could spray it anywhere they thought the monsters would come from, and it would keep them away. It got a little wet, but everyone got more sleep, so I was okay with that."
—*Brooke Kuhns, Dayton, OH*

"I have created a superhero just for my child. He is available on demand to fight off any scary monsters, etc."
—*Rachel Hampton-Saint, Kent, England*

"Validate their feelings. Always to them, it's real. I try to keep them from seeing things that may scare them—TV, movies, etc. If they are scared at night or have a bad dream, I'll lie with them and either read them a good story or try to get their minds on something nice."
—*Missi Darnell, Acton, CA*

CHAPTER SIXTEEN

READY
FOR ANOTHER ONE?

You've got experience on your side. But every conception, pregnancy, and baby is different. And this time, you've also got one or more kids to take care of while you're pregnant. Here's how to get pregnant and enjoy it the next time around.

Our Four Best Tips When Trying to Conceive and It's Taking Longer than Expected

1. Do whatever you can to relax. Whether it means taking a special yoga class, praying, meditating, or exercising, it will help.
2. Have sex every other day.
3. Elevate your pelvis after intercourse.
4. Get help quickly (within six months).

"I am a big believer in not waiting if there are infertility problems, and don't let your OB waste your money and use up your insurance. Go to a fertility specialist. OBs are busy doing exams, pap smears, etc. Your fertility doctor's only goal is to get you pregnant."
—*Andrea Suissa, Olney, MD*

"Try to relax! As difficult as that is, the stress you place on yourself can actually be keeping you from conceiving. Our mental state has a lot to do with the physical state of our bodies. The chemicals your body releases when stressed, anxious, or depressed will interfere with your body's ability to conceive.

"It also helped me to remember that God had just the right baby in mind for our family. If I had become pregnant any other month, we would have had different egg and sperm and would have gotten a different baby. The three we have are just perfect for our family."
—Angela Snodgrass, Meridian, ID

"We were trying for close to a year before I got pregnant, and the only thing that seems to work is the same thing that is almost impossible to do when you're actively trying to have a baby: relax, don't think about it, and just have fun. It's very true that when you stop trying is when it happens."
—K. Scarlett Shaw, Euless, TX

"After we had intercourse, I would prop my hips up on two pillows and stay like that for thirty minutes. I did it for about two weeks and it worked after two years of trying doing nothing."
—Amanda Marbrey, Dyersburg, TN

"It took us over a year to get pregnant, and we went through a fertility specialist. It was the month that we decided not to do all the ovulation predictors and tried just to have fun that I finally got pregnant. I also had read somewhere that after intercourse, if you lie down for a while with your pelvis elevated that it helps the sperm move along, and we did do that the month I got pregnant."
—Traci Bragg, M.D., Jacksonville, FL

"Have intercourse every other day from day ten to day twenty of your cycle."
—Kimberly Mercurio, M.D., Downers Grove, IL

Five Smart Ways to Take Care of Yourself When You Are Pregnant and Have Little One(s) in Tow

1. Rest as much as possible: Nap when the kids nap, and sleep when they sleep.
2. Accept help.
3. Schedule time for yourself on a regular basis.
4. Pamper yourself.
5. Spend time with the older child(ren).

"Now that I am pregnant with my third child, the best advice I can offer is to try and relax and rest when the kids are napping or watching a video. If I am rested, I can deal with everything much better. I also have a babysitter every Friday, which gives me a little alone time, and I love it."
—*Ann Stowe, Burlingame, CA*

"The best way to take of yourself when you're pregnant and have other children is to eat right, get sleep when your other children rest, and don't make a supermom out of yourself."
—*Patricia Hale, Hanover, MD*

"The single most important thing to do for yourself is ask for help! You will need as much rest as you can get, and now is the perfect time to allow others to help you out with their time. Perhaps they could bring you frozen, home-prepared meals in ready-to-heat-and-serve portions. Or offer to help by taking your little one(s) off your hands for a short time, so you can get either a nap in or even get some shopping done."
—*Lisa Bittar, Brooklyn, NY*

"Get plenty of rest, sleep when your other children sleep. Go for a walk with them. Try to fix them healthier snacks/meals, so you can eat healthy also."
—*Debby Madrid, Elkhart, IN*

Breaking the News to Your Kids That a New Baby Is on the Way

1. Keep your child(ren)'s age(s) in mind. Don't break the news to a two-year-old when you're only two months pregnant.
2. Give the child a sense of ownership of the baby.
3. Show him that he will have a new role in the family.

"Wait as long as you can to tell them because nine months can seem like an eternity to a young child. When the new baby is born, have a gift from the baby to the sibling(s)."
—*Keli Loveland, Bartlett, TN*

"Just tell them. It also helps to refer to the baby as 'your baby' to your toddler so that they get a sense of responsibility that they will help with the baby, too. It also will help them not feel that they are no longer mommy and daddy's baby but will be replaced by the new baby—the new baby can be called [toddler's name]'s baby."
—*Kari Rydell, Ladera Ranch, CA*

"I told my son that I had another baby in my tummy and he would be a big brother. We told him how important the role of a big brother was. I also bought him a baby doll so he could practice feeding and holding the baby."
—*Denine Scallen, Sammamish, WA*

The Top Ten Ways You Know You've Become a Mom

THEY SAY THAT ONCE YOU HAVE A BABY, your life will never be the same. We can't argue with that. What they don't tell you is that your whole vocabulary, the very definitions of words and phrases, changes, too. Here are just a few of the phrases that took on new meaning when we became moms:

1. ENTERTAINING
Before We Became Moms: Hosting a dinner party for twelve, complete with appetizers, fine wine, sparkling conversation, and a flaming dessert.
After We Became Moms: Having eight sixteen-month-olds and their moms over for playgroup, during which your toddler's toys are "explored" by eight new sets of gums, and you are reprimanded for not putting protective coating around the sharp corners of your coffee table.

2. WORKING OUT
Before We Became Moms: Going to a gym or fitness center or engaging in a sport or activity for at least a half hour with the goal of burning calories, building muscles, and/or losing weight.

After We Became Moms: Chasing our toddlers up and down the stairs twelve times an hour with the goal of avoiding a trip to the emergency room.

3. RELAXING
Before We Became Moms: Treating ourselves to a spa day, complete with massage, facial, manicure, and pedicure.
After We Became Moms: Being allowed to sleep for more than two hours without interruption.

4. VACATION
Before We Became Moms: Jetting off to an exotic island with your sweetheart to soak up the sun, splash in the surf, and dance your cares away until the sun comes up.
After We Became Moms: Feeding, changing, and cleaning up after your child(ren) somewhere other than your own house—in other words, a change in scenery.

5. BEST GUILT-FREE INDULGENCE
Before We Became Moms: Nonfat Häagan-Dazs
After We Became Moms: Baby Einstein videos

6. SNACK
Before We Became Moms: Rice cakes and a decaf, nonfat, double latte.
After We Became Moms: Half a plate of macaroni and cheese left over from our toddler's lunch, plus the half-full bag of Teddy Grahams found at the bottom of the diaper bag, and washed down with a double, full-caf mocha with extra whipped cream.

7. DREAM DATE
Before We Became Moms: A candlelit dinner in an elegant restaurant followed by a romantic stroll on the beach.

TO CONTRIBUTE TO THE NEXT EDITION,
VISIT WWW.GALLAGHERGUIDE.COM

After We Became Moms: Any dinner that: a) we don't have to prepare, b) we don't have to clean up, and c) does not require us to talk into a speaker to order. We'll skip the romantic stroll (who needs sand in her panty hose anyway?) if we get to stay in our seats through the entire meal and finish at least two sentences without being interrupted.

8. GOOD LUCK

Before We Became Moms: Winning the lottery.

After We Became Moms: Arriving at the photography studio and realizing that your baby's outfit is *still* free of all spit-up, poopy, and jelly stains.

9. SUCCESSFUL SHOPPING TRIP

Before We Became Moms: Spending an entire Saturday with a girlfriend scouring the off-price stores, outlets, and designer boutique sales and scoring a Prada handbag for 50 percent off retail.

After We Became Moms: Prada who? Going to Target at 9:30 p.m. BY OURSELVES and discovering that Pampers are on sale.

10. LOVE

Before We Became Moms: A wonderful feeling arising from being with an attractive person, who makes your heart swell.

After We Became Moms: A wonderful feeling arising from being with a short, fat, toothless person who makes your heart swell.

MEET OUR CONTRIBUTING AUTHORS

ANGELA ANDERSON lives in Seattle, WA with her husband, Ron, and her son, Sam. An attorney, she enjoys running and reading in her spare time.

DESHAWN ANDERSON-DREW is currently residing in Apopka, FL while completing her internship at the Florida College of Integrative Medicine. In her free time, she enjoys spending time with family and Israeli folk dancing.

SYLVIA ANDERSON lives in Rapid City, SD with her husband and son, Adam. She is currently studying at the University of South Dakota School of Medicine and, as such, is chronically tired and always looking for shortcuts.

Based in Spokane, WA, **BOBBI ANNAL** and her husband, Joe, have two daughters, Ceaira and Kailyn. When not busy trying to keep her household sane and her girls in one piece, she enjoys scrapbooking, crocheting, drawing, and learning the new things that life has to offer.

PATRICIA ARNOLD lives in Westford, MA with her husband and toddler twins. She fondly remembers the days when she enjoyed crafts, traveling, and conversations that did not involve the mention of bodily functions.

DANA BAEDKE lives in Chalfont, PA with her daughters, Mackenzie, Kelsey, and Riley, and her husband, Sean. She works full-time as a marketing communications manager for a high-tech company.

RACHEL BAILEY lives in Bay Minette, AL with her husband, Samuel, her daughter, Samantha, and her baby son, Connor. She is the owner and director of Adventures in Childcare and Learning, a child care center.

From Bettendorf, IA, **JULIE BARTLETT** is a stay-at-home mom of two daughters, Eliza, eight, and Sarah, five. She is active in her church on the wellness committee, in Ministry of Moms Sharing (MOMS), and on the planning committee for Children's Liturgy of the Word.

DIANE BEDROSIAN, M.D., lives in Carlsbad, CA with her daughters, ages five and three. She works part-time as a pediatrician, and when not spending time with her daughters, she enjoys running at the beach and hiking.

JANA BELL lives in London, OH with her husband, Ric, and two sons, Casey and Christopher. She is a part-time automation coordinator at a small public library. Her hobbies include reading, cooking, and catching catnaps whenever possible!

MAYA BENELI lives in Carmichael, CA with her two-year-old daughter. She has been a single mom since her daughter was three months old.

SUSAN BENOVITZ lives in Gaithersburg, MD with her husband, Eric, and sons, Gabriel and Simon. A dental hygienist by trade, she hopes to practice again in a few years.

Stay-at-home mom, **MELISSA BEST** and her husband, Jim, live in Southwestern Pennsylvania with their daughter, Abigail. She enjoys reading, scrapbooking, and crafts.

TARA BETTERIDGE lives in Fort Lewis, WA with her husband, David, and son, Nicolae. She is a teacher at a day care center.

CLAIRE BIENVENU, PH.D., lives in Slidell, LA with her husband, Frank Spiess, and their daughter, Vivienne. She is a college administrator and licensed professional counselor who enjoys life's simple blessings and pleasures.

Single mom **LISA BITTAR** (a.k.a. Superwoman) is raising her three awesome children: Timothy Joseph, Tyler Dylan, and Madyson Rene in Brooklyn, NY. For her, instilling traditions and family values in the children are what's most important.

Menlo Park, CA is home to **BETH BLECHERMAN,** her son, Benjamin, and husband, Neil. Her favorite leisure activities used to be reading fiction and exercising. Now she reads parenting books and gets her exercise trying to keep up with her son.

DESIREE BOCHMAN and her husband live in Paradise, CA with their son, Curtis. She says, "As a mother, I strive to maintain a balance in my marriage while raising my son. I also feel that it is extremely important for us as mothers to remember that we need to make time for ourselves."

COLLEEN BOUCHARD and her husband, Steve, have two daughters, Emma and Eleanor. Based in Bel Air, MD, Colleen is a graphic

TO CONTRIBUTE TO THE NEXT EDITION, VISIT WWW.GALLAGHERGUIDE.COM

designer who runs two businesses: Cool Baby Graphics and Tickle Bellies.

TRACI BRAGG, M.D., has twin boys and works as a family medicine physician in Jacksonville, FL. She loves spending time with her family, playing outside, going to the park, and reading to her kids.

JENNIFER BRANNON lives in Huntington Beach, CA with her husband, Brian, baby Isabella, and their two dogs. She is a full-time communications manager for a software company.

KEL BRIGHT lives in Charleston, SC with her husband, son, Ashton, two cats, a dog, and a hamster. She likes to read, go to the beach, and do scrapbooking.

LISA BROOKS lives in Butler, PA with her husband, Rob, and sons, Andre, eight months, and Micah, eight years. A stay-at-home mom and homeschooler, Lisa works part-time at home doing computer work and selling on eBay.

JACLYN "ANGEL" BROUSSARD lives in Lake Charles, LA with her husband, Shelley Paul, and their daughter, Juliana Isabella. She is a stay-at-home mom whose interests include running after her daughter, shopping, and spending time with her family.

Currently residing in Kapolei, HI, **BRENDA BROWN** is a full-time mother and very part-time housekeeper. Her best parenting advice is, "Follow your heart."

MELANIE BRYANT-KELSEY has one child and lives in Edison, NJ.

LORI BURGESS is a wife, mother of four young children, home manager, chef, organizing guru, and entertainment/activities director. In addition, she and her husband manage and maintain the family's business enterprises out of their home in Maine.

CRYSTAL BURRISS lives in Raleigh, NC with her husband, Michael, and baby, Joshua. She is a new stay-at-home mom who enjoys cooking, shopping, and volunteering.

MICHELE CARLON, M.D., is a physician in private practice in Oak Park, IL. She lives in Chicago with her husband, Juan, and two rambunctious children, Tommy and Ellie.

Tulsa, OK-based **BRANDY CHARLES** is a mom who enjoys spending her free time with her son and husband. Her favorite quote is: "Rest? What's that?"

LEAH CHEW lives in Tucker, GA with her two sons, Kieran and Onan, and her wonderful, helping husband, Frank.

ELIZA LO CHIN, M.D., is a part-time general internist and mother of three. She is also the editor of *This Side of Doctoring: Reflections from Women in Medicine,* an intimate collection of stories, essays, and poems by women physicians. She lives in Piedmont, CA.

The proud deaf mom of hearing children who speak sign language, **CONNIE CHOATE** lives in Gardner, KS with her four kids and her husband, Jeff. In her free time, she enjoys cooking and traveling.

DEBBIE CLARK has two children and lives in Charlotte, NC.

A pediatric nurse by profession, **HOLLY COCCHIOLA** now enjoys being a stay-at-home mom to Liam, two, and the family's newest edition, Chase. They live in Bethlehem, CT.

KATIE CONROY lives in Palos Hills, IL with husband, Mike, two-year-old comedian, Brendan, and the family's newest additions, twins Aidan Thomas and Devin Michael. When she's not coaching the members of her "all-male mini rugby team," Katie enjoys small bouts of peace and quiet.

Work-at-home mom **DANA A. CROY** lives in Murfreesboro, TN with her husband, Nathan, and son, Noah. An avid supporter of attachment parenting, she works as a trainer/event coordinator for a local bookstore.

REBECCA CURTIS lives in Oshawa, Ontario, Canada with her husband, Albert, and children, Zachary and Savannah. Her parenting philosophy is, "It isn't about luck in parenting, birth, or hockey. It's about skill and patience. And a little pain tolerance never hurt either."

KAREN CUTCHIN lives in Portland, ME with her son, Benjamin. She enjoys the rare nap and trying out different foods on her son to watch the faces.

DARYL D'ANGELO lives in Sewell, NJ with her husband, John, and daughters, Jordan, Jenna, and Carly. She enjoys cooking, decorating, and the beach.

MISSI DARNELL lives in Acton, CA with her husband, Kirk, and five children, Nicholas, Rachel, Olivia, Genevieve, and Michael. She enjoys raising her children, genealogy, and the outdoors.

DONNA DAVIDSON lives in Weymouth, MA with her husband, Don, daughter, Madeline, and son, Ryan. She works full-time and enjoys spending time with her family, scrapbooking, and catching up on sleep when she is not working.

Gaithersburg, MD is home to **KIM DELPRETE,** her husband, Wayne, and daughters, Alexa, Tara, and Jodi. Her passions include cooking and playing mah-jongg.

A full-time dermatologist, **BRENDA DINTIMAN, M.D.,** lives in Fairfax, VA with her husband and two children, Christine, thirteen, and Teddy, ten. When not working, you can find her gardening, playing tennis, or carting her kids to tennis, soccer, drama, and voice lessons.

SARA DIXON lives in Grimesland, NC with her husband, Mark, and their children, Courtney, Haley, and Taylor, and the family dog, Hero. Her oldest daughter, Caitlyn, lives in heaven. She is an RN who works full-time and treasures every moment (well, most moments) spent with her family.

SUSAN DOBRATZ and her husband live in Plymouth, MA with daughter, Reagan, and son, Cameron. Until last year, she was a stay-at-home mom. Now she works as a preschool director. Her only wish is that her kids wouldn't grow so fast.

WENDY DOUGLAS lives in Margate, FL with her husband, Donnie and her "little men," AJ, Conner, and Zachary. A stay-at-home mom, her hobbies are reading, watching movies, and chatting with her mommies' group friends.

VALERIE DOWNS and her husband, Jason, live in Altoona, PA where she is a stay-at-home mom to her son, Alexander. In her free time, she loves to talk to other mothers about the joys and struggles that come with raising children.

Stay-at-home mom **ALEJANDRA DOZAL** lives in El Paso, TX with her husband, Roberto Dozal, Sr., and children, Paulette, Giovanna, and Roberto, Jr. She says, "The best part of being a mom is having an excuse to go see a PG movie."

At-home mom **CAROLYN DUNN** lives in Morristown, NJ with her husband and son. She is president of the MOMS Club of East Hanover Area, NJ and is in the process of founding a new chapter in Morristown. A freelance editor, she enjoys reading, exercising, and working on scrapbooks in her free time.

JEANNETTE ESHBACH lives in Roy, UT with her daughter, Dani, Dani's boyfriend, John, and their son, Steven. Two other daughters live close by, Mandy and husband Kyle, Latishia and Mike, and their two daughters, Skylynn and Lillie. Her daughter, Felicia, is her guardian angel.

DEBBIE EZRIN lives in Gaithersburg, MD with her husband, Mark, and her two children, Melanie and Jared.

SALLY FARRINGTON lives in Fayetteville, NC with her three beautiful daughters and military husband, Dave. She enjoys reading, gardening, church, and hugging her three daughters!

JONALEE FERNATT resides in Ulrichsville, OH with her husband, Mike, and son, Braden. Jonalee currently works part-time at an appraisal firm. Her hobbies include trying to play the piano, nursing her son, trying to cook dinner, nursing her son, trying to get sleep, and nursing her son.

SARAH FOX is an obsessive and overanalyzing mother of princess Zoie and daily challenges Ben and Sam. She and her extremely patient husband, Ray, house the clan in Fort Collins, CO. Sarah is a senior environmental planner and when she isn't working or managing the household circus, she enjoys trying to figure out how she got to where she is today.

HEATHER FRENCH is thrilled to be raising her amazing son, Liam, in Fishers, IN with her extraordinary husband, Jason. She manages this honor as well as working full-time. In her spare time she loves crafts and sewing, as well as participating in Liam's day care PTO, striving to make things at his day care as wonderful as possible for him and the other children.

JESSICA GANE lives in Brookhaven, PA with her daughter. She spends her free time fire fighting and doing ambulance work.

BECKY GASTON lives in Owensboro, KY with her daughter, Haleigh Marie, and husband, Nathan. She enjoys taking long walks with her toddler and taking her to the zoo and the pool. She is also a full-time law student.

Emergency Medicine Resident **MICHELLE GEBHARD, D.O.,** lives in White Plains, NY with her daughter, Sabine, and husband, Kai. She tries to find something great about every scenario she encounters in life.

JANETTE GILMAN lives in Potomac, MD with her husband, Peter, her son, Sam, and her daughter, Adele. A full-time government economic analyst, a fun-time basket consultant, and an elementary school room mom, she believes in keeping the gas tank at least half full at all times.

DAYNA LAWSON GILMORE lives in The Woodlands, TX with her husband, Barry, and children, Laura, Matthew, and Nathan. She enjoys the computer, children, and writing.

ANITA GOOD lives in Hewitt, NJ with her son, Ryan, and her husband, Charlie. They enjoy family time, which usually involves Play-Doh or movie nights with popcorn.

GAIL VOLD GRECO has one child and lives in Minneapolis, MN.

ROBYN GREENHOUSE lives in Gaithersburg, MD with her husband, Stephen, and sons, Ryan, Tyler, and Dylan. In her free time, she enjoys running, reading, and cooking.

MARLO GREENSPAN lives in Boyds, MD with her husband, Ira, and daughter, Leah. She enjoys being with children, playing word games, writing/editing, and singing (as long as no one is listening!).

A full-time mother of two boys, a new wife, and solo practitioner in a breast and general surgical practice, **DENISE GREENWOOD, M.D.,** lives the life that she has always sworn was possible. Her favorite quote is, "How could anyone ever tell us that we can't have it all?!"

ANGE GREGORY lives in Stanwood, IA with her husband, Bob, daughter, Bethany, and son, Patrick. She works as the community administrator for BabyCenter.com. In her spare time (oops—what is that, again?), she enjoys reading, cross-stitching, and scrapbooking.

SHANNON GUAY lives in Galloway, OH with her husband, Christopher, and their two daughters, Christina and Stephanie. She currently works part-time and enjoys spending time with family and friends. In her free time, she likes to read, listen to music, and take relaxing baths.

KATIE ANNE GUSTAFSSON lives in Eskilstuna, Sweden with her soul mate/husband, Mikael, and their two adorable boys, Jakob and Connor. Although a freelance writer, part-time student (and professional procrastinator), Katie Anne puts family at the top of her priority list.

KAREN HAAS lives in Laurel, MD with her two children and her husband, Mark. She enjoys entertaining friends and family at her home, vacationing at the beach, and attending her children's many sporting events.

JENNA HALDEMAN lives in Portland, OR with her husband, Mark, and their sixteen-month-old twins, Michael and Jack. A full-time mommy,

Jenna is also a full-time athlete, competing in several marathons and distance relays a year. She is always in search of the next challenge and the next bowl of cookie dough ice cream!

A Baltimore County, MD public school teacher, **PATRICIA HALE** loves teaching and raising her children, Matt and Bethany, with her husband, Mike. Her hobbies include spring planting, collecting angels, and nature.

KATE HALLBERG lives in Boulder, CO with her three children, her husband, Dirk, a University of Colorado professor, and dear dog and cats. She enjoys hiking, skiing, camping, and brewing beer, and has never been sleep deprived because the family cosleeps. She is on the pathway to becoming a certified lactation consultant and birth doula as soon as possible.

SARAH HALLBERG, M.D., is a physician who lives in Indianapolis, IN with her stay-at-home husband, Brad, and son, Noah. She enjoys anything and everything with her family and also politics and cooking.

CHELSEA HAMMAN, M.D., lives in Providence, NC with her husband, Jonathan, and daughter, Faith. She is a resident physician in family medicine at Moses Cone Hospital in Greensboro, NC. In her (sometimes rare) free time, she enjoys spending time with her family doing such things as hiking, camping, and going to the zoo.

SARA HAMMONTREE lives in Mountain Home, AR with her son, Joseph, her husband, Ryan, and several dogs and cats. She enjoys kayaking, rappelling, scrapbooking, dancing with Joseph, and learning how to show dogs.

RACHEL HAMPTON-SAINT lives in Kent, England with her husband, Alex, and sons, Gabriel and Ollie. A full-time university worker, she tries to fit in another life as a full-time mom, chef, family personal assistant, and social worker!

A stay-at-home mommy and very proud army wife, **KELLY HARDEN** lives in Fort Hood, TX with her son, Dylan, and husband, Ed. Her hobbies include scrapbooking, dancing, time with her family and friends, and counting the days until Ed gets home from his deployment to Iraq.

Rhode Island native **REBECCA HARPER** currently lives in Gaston, SC with her significant other, Art, their two sons, Michael and Jordan, and Art's daughter, Emily. Her favorite leisure-time activities are reading and sleeping.

HEATHER HENDRICKSON lives in Yucaipa, CA with her husband, Nick, and son, Chance. She enjoys spending time with her family, redecorating her house, and going to local MOMS Club functions.

ELIZABETH HILDEBRAND is a first-time mother who lives in Greenville, PA with her husband, Nick, and daughter, Ella. She has two full-time occupations: mother and public relations professional. She is an expert in nursing, diaper changing, bottlefeeding, burping, and cleaning up various baby messes. In her spare time, she enjoys sleeping.

SHELLY SOLOMON HUGGINS, ED.D., lives in Bel Air, MD with her husband, Matt, and daughter, Kristin. She has a doctorate in education and works as an assistant professor in the elementary childhood department at Towson University.

RACHEL HULAN lives in Lake Forest, CA with her wonderful husband, Ron, and her amazing son, Grant. She is discovering every day what a joy it is to be a mother.

JAMIE HUNLEY lives in San Diego, CA with her husband, Michael, daughter Skylar, two dogs, three cats, and one bird. When not running Skylar back and forth between preschool, ballet, the park, and swimming, the Hunleys operate a concession business.

KAREN HURST resides in Roseville, CA with her wonderful husband, Darren, and their beautiful daughter, Sydney. Karen is an aspiring college instructor in business management and is currently an Internet-based business owner, creating custom jewelry for moms (www.charmingdesigns.com).

ANNA MARIA JOHNSON lives in Shreveport, LA with her husband, Mike, son, Payne, and newborn son, Peyton. "Being a mother to two precious boys is the most wonderful thing in the world. I love them so much," she says. "I am so happy to have been able to contribute to this book and to share my experiences with other mothers."

HANNAH CHOW JOHNSON, M.D., is a pediatrician in North Riverside, IL. She lives in Elmhurst, IL with her husband, Frank, and sons, William and Alexander. Someday she hopes to write a book on toilet training based on her personal and professional experiences.

KRYSTAL JOHNSTON, M.D., lives in Manistee, MI with her husband, Nick, and their energetic son, Bryce. She has a growing pediatric practice and enjoys many craft projects in her scant free time.

DODI KINGSFIELD is a career mom living in Forestville, NY with her stay-at-home husband, Bill, and five children. Son, Cassidy, and daughters, Madeleine, Phoebe, Clare, and Winnifred all add to the excitement and chaos of everyday life in the Kingsfield household.

Oncologist **DAWN KIRNON, M.D.,** lives in New York City. She is the cofounder of a Cancer Resource Center in New York with her partner in life and business, Albert Aldrich, Jr. She has three amazing daughters and enjoys traveling and going to Broadway shows, museums, and concerts.

Stay-at-home mom **MARI KISTLER** lives in St. Petersburg, FL with her husband, Nathan, and her son. She enjoys keeping her local Starbucks in business as well as thinking of what she would do if she had more free time.

SHELLY KNIGHT lives in Longmont, CO with her husband, Rob, daughter, Emily, and cat, Charlie. She works part-time and enjoys camping and hiking with her husband and daughter.

AMY KOBLER lives in Buffalo, NY with her husband, Dave, son, Jacob, and daughter, Sarah. She is a stay-at-home mom who never seems to be home! Her hobbies include gardening, volunteering at her children's school, and enjoying activities with them.

KATIE KROLL lives in Smyrna, GA with her husband, David, and baby daughter, Ella. A stay-at-home mom, she enjoys finishing her thoughts in her spare time.

AMY KUBECKA, her husband, Mark, and daughter, Avery, raise fish on a farm in Palacios, TX. When not busy being a mother and wife of a fish farmer, Amy works part-time at her premommy job as a geographic information systems specialist for a firm in Houston.

Dayton, OH-based **BROOKE KUHNS** and her husband, Sean, have four sons, Caleb, Bailey, Zachary, and Seth. A full-time secretary with a local business newspaper, her hobbies are reading Stephen King novels and sleeping all night. Unfortunately, she doesn't get much chance to enjoy either of these hobbies.

SABRINA LANE lives in Boise, ID with her husband, David, and her two beautiful daughters, Mercedes and Tapanga. In her free time, she can be found curled up on the couch with a good book.

MICHELLE LANEY is a stay-at-home mom living in Helena, AL with her husband, David, and their two daughters. Their family is soon to grow with the upcoming arrival of their third daughter.

CHANTAL LAURIN enjoys singing, dancing, and spending time with her daughter, Erika. Chantal and husband, Jeff, cannot imagine life without her! And now they are looking forward to welcoming a new baby to their family. They live in Concord, Ontario, Canada.

BRANDI LEACH lives in Fort Worth, TX with her husband, Frank, and daughter, Alexia (nicknamed Alex). She is a stay-at-home mom who likes to read in her spare time.

KERITH LEFFLER lives in Morristown, NJ with her husband, Brad, and daughters, Kirsten and Katelyn. She is a stay-at-home mom who enjoys scrapbooking, church activities, traveling, and sleeping.

JAIMELIN LIDDELL lives in Roseto, PA. She has one child.

EVA LINDSEY lives in Dallas, TX with her husband, Michael, and two sons, Gage and Caden. A full-time working mom, she loves to chase her kids and dream of a month-long vacation in Hawaii.

LINDA LINGUVIC lives in New York City. The mother of two grown children and the grandmother of two toddlers, she works as an administrative coordinator at a large, nonprofit organization and writes a daily e-mail column. She visits her grandchildren once a week and enjoys seeing the world through their eyes.

KARI LOMANNO lives in Chesapeake, VA with her husband, Jeff, daughter, Samantha, and son, Miles. She enjoys spending time with her family, freelance writing, and selling Avon.

SUSAN LONERGAN resides in Woodside, CA with her two children who are under the age of five, two children who are in college, and a very wise husband who, after having four children, is an expert in being a "mommy," too.

MICHELE LONGENBACH lives in Garden Grove, CA with her husband, Roger, and son, Robbie. She works from home as a medical transcriptionist.

KELI LOVELAND, husband, David, and their three girls, Shelby, Avery, and Riley, live in Bartlett, TN. Keli can be found at her local recreation complex, her "second home," from April through October, playing softball and working in the concession stand. She is also a soccer coach, amateur photographer, and loves to try to scrapboo' the photos of her family.

SUSAN LOWRY lives in Mooresville, IN with her husband, Jerr' son, Xander. She enjoys reading, web surfing, and shopping!

DEBBY MADRID lives in Elkhart, IN with her husband, Jorge, and two daughters, Madison and Jordan. She is a stay-at-home mom and enjoys each and every day with her children.

AMANDA MARBREY, husband, Michael, and daughter, Alexis Faith, live in Dyersburg, TN. In her spare time, she enjoys going for walks, fishing, or doing something quiet and peaceful with her husband.

A former language arts teacher who is currently homeschooling her children, **DANIELLE MARION-DOYLE** lives in Donaldsonville, LA with her husband, Tim, and their children, Adam and Nicole, five. Some of her favorite pastimes include reading, crocheting, and taking family vacations on the spur of the moment.

SIDNEY MARKS lives in Menlo Park, CA with her husband, their three children, and the family dog. She is a stay-at-home mom and thrives on the chaos of family life with three little ones.

MEGAN MARTIN lives in Crystal Lake, IL with her husband, Lance, two-and-a-half-year-old daughter, Halle, and newborn son, Connor. She is a full-time mom and is a firm believer in the adage, "The only perfect parent is the one with no children."

STEPHANIE MARTIN lives in Macomb, MI with her husband, Lynn, sons, Philip, William, and daughter, Lillian. This full-time stay-at-home mom can be found diving into the latest mystery novel, cooking, or scrapbooking when she's not tending to her greatest joy, her family.

AAMINA MASOOD lives with her husband, Ahsan Ale-Rasool, and daughter, Aaishah, in Richardson, TX. She is a web developer and full-time mom, who occasionally does volunteer work from home.

Sartell, MN is home to **KRISTEN MATH,** her four children, an Australian shepherd and her husband, Thomas. She currently teaches biology part-time at her local state university. She is also the founder of medicalspouse.org, a website community providing support to the spouses of physicians.

Stay-at-home mom **DAFNI MAUCHLEY** has four boys, Dakota, Dausen, Dalton, and Dallas. She also has three stepdaughters, Keri, Erika, and Tawny. She and her husband, Shaun, have been married for three years. They live in Phelan, CA.

Kinnelon, NJ-based mom, **TAMMY MCCLUSKEY, M.D.,** works part-time in a busy, two-pediatrician practice in order to participate actively in the lives of her two young children.

CHANTAL LAURIN enjoys singing, dancing, and spending time with her daughter, Erika. Chantal and husband, Jeff, cannot imagine life without her! And now they are looking forward to welcoming a new baby to their family. They live in Concord, Ontario, Canada.

BRANDI LEACH lives in Fort Worth, TX with her husband, Frank, and daughter, Alexia (nicknamed Alex). She is a stay-at-home mom who likes to read in her spare time.

KERITH LEFFLER lives in Morristown, NJ with her husband, Brad, and daughters, Kirsten and Katelyn. She is a stay-at-home mom who enjoys scrapbooking, church activities, traveling, and sleeping.

JAIMELIN LIDDELL lives in Roseto, PA. She has one child.

EVA LINDSEY lives in Dallas, TX with her husband, Michael, and two sons, Gage and Caden. A full-time working mom, she loves to chase her kids and dream of a month-long vacation in Hawaii.

LINDA LINGUVIC lives in New York City. The mother of two grown children and the grandmother of two toddlers, she works as an administrative coordinator at a large, nonprofit organization and writes a daily e-mail column. She visits her grandchildren once a week and enjoys seeing the world through their eyes.

KARI LOMANNO lives in Chesapeake, VA with her husband, Jeff, daughter, Samantha, and son, Miles. She enjoys spending time with her family, freelance writing, and selling Avon.

SUSAN LONERGAN resides in Woodside, CA with her two children who are under the age of five, two children who are in college, and a very wise husband who, after having four children, is an expert in being a "mommy," too.

MICHELE LONGENBACH lives in Garden Grove, CA with her husband, Roger, and son, Robbie. She works from home as a medical transcriptionist.

KELI LOVELAND, husband, David, and their three girls, Shelby, Avery, and Riley, live in Bartlett, TN. Keli can be found at her local recreation complex, her "second home," from April through October, playing softball and working in the concession stand. She is also a soccer coach, amateur photographer, and loves to try to scrapboo' the photos of her family.

SUSAN LOWRY lives in Mooresville, IN with her husband, Jerr' son, Xander. She enjoys reading, web surfing, and shopping!

DEBBY MADRID lives in Elkhart, IN with her husband, Jorge, and two daughters, Madison and Jordan. She is a stay-at-home mom and enjoys each and every day with her children.

AMANDA MARBREY, husband, Michael, and daughter, Alexis Faith, live in Dyersburg, TN. In her spare time, she enjoys going for walks, fishing, or doing something quiet and peaceful with her husband.

A former language arts teacher who is currently homeschooling her children, **DANIELLE MARION-DOYLE** lives in Donaldsonville, LA with her husband, Tim, and their children, Adam and Nicole, five. Some of her favorite pastimes include reading, crocheting, and taking family vacations on the spur of the moment.

SIDNEY MARKS lives in Menlo Park, CA with her husband, their three children, and the family dog. She is a stay-at-home mom and thrives on the chaos of family life with three little ones.

MEGAN MARTIN lives in Crystal Lake, IL with her husband, Lance, two-and-a-half-year-old daughter, Halle, and newborn son, Connor. She is a full-time mom and is a firm believer in the adage, "The only perfect parent is the one with no children."

STEPHANIE MARTIN lives in Macomb, MI with her husband, Lynn, sons, Philip, William, and daughter, Lillian. This full-time stay-at-home mom can be found diving into the latest mystery novel, cooking, or scrapbooking when she's not tending to her greatest joy, her family.

AAMINA MASOOD lives with her husband, Ahsan Ale-Rasool, and daughter, Aaishah, in Richardson, TX. She is a web developer and full-time mom, who occasionally does volunteer work from home.

Sartell, MN is home to **KRISTEN MATH,** her four children, an Australian shepherd and her husband, Thomas. She currently teaches biology part-time at her local state university. She is also the founder of medicalspouse.org, a website community providing support to the spouses of physicians.

Stay-at-home mom **DAFNI MAUCHLEY** has four boys, Dakota, Dausen, Dalton, and Dallas. She also has three stepdaughters, Keri, Erika, and Tawny. She and her husband, Shaun, have been married for three years. They live in Phelan, CA.

Kinnelon, NJ-based mom, **TAMMY MCCLUSKEY, M.D.,** works part-time in a busy, two-pediatrician practice in order to participate actively in the lives of her two young children.

APRIL MCCONNELL lives in Birdsboro, PA with her husband, Mark, daughter, Taylor Paige, and son, Ethan Brady. She is a stay-at-home mom and enjoys spending time with her family.

AMY MCDONALD lives in Buffalo, MN with her husband, Jeff, son, Ross, and dogs, Spud and Doozi. In her spare time, she enjoys reading and working out.

Working full-time in television news, **LISA MCDONALD** lives in Maitland, FL (just outside of Orlando) with her husband, Andy, a radio engineer, and son, Maximilian Kain. She enjoys playing with her son, taking long, hot baths, and writing fantasy, horror, and science fiction.

SUZANNE MCMILLAN lives in Greenbrier, TN with her husband, John, son, Cole, and baby number two on the way. As an interior designer and fitness instructor, Suzanne's life as a mommy has changed both her home and her figure, but she loves them anyway!

HEATHER MEININGER lives in Charlotte, NC with her husband, Kevin, and daughter, Caroline Grace. She runs a website for mothers in Charlotte and also enjoys reading, writing, and volunteering at her church.

ANNA MARIE MENTA lives in Clifton Heights, PA with her husband, Jon, son, Jonathan, and daughter, Kathryn. She is a stay-at-home mom who misses sleep desperately, but feels it's well worth it.

KIMBERLY MERCURIO, M.D., is currently a stay-at-home mom residing in Downers Grove, IL with her husband, Jim, and three children. She enjoys scrapbooking, reading, and playing tennis when she is not chauffeuring, nursing, or playing kitchen.

A single working mother, **BECKY MESSERLI** lives in Chesterfield, MI with her son, Wesley. A legal assistant by day, she pulls out her cape at night and becomes Supermom . . . faster than a speeding toddler, more powerful than diaper rash, and able to leap tall toys in a single bound.

Marysville, WA is home to **MEGAN MILES,** her husband, and three children. She loves her career as a Tupperware manager, which allows her the flexibility to stay at home with her children—or to spend her days shuttling between school, sports, dance, and all the other activities that come with a preteen, a preschooler, and a new baby.

BETH MILLER lives in Novato, CA with her son, Sam, and husband, Steve. She and Sam love going for walks every day with friends,

because fresh air can make a world of difference to a stressed-out mom and baby.

DIANA MOLAVI, M.D., PH.D, lives in Baltimore, MD with her husband, Rameen, and their two daughters, Claire and Annelise. As a two-physician family, they rely heavily on nearby family and minimalistic survival strategies. Pets, hobbies, and elaborate meals are on hold until Diana finishes her residency.

GENEVIEVE MOLLOY lives in Guttenberg, NJ with her daughter, Sophia, and husband, Tommy. After staying home with her daughter for two-and-a-half years, she is now pursuing a three-day-a-week career.

DONNICA MOORE, M.D., lives in Branchburg, NJ with her husband and two school-aged children. A noted women's health expert, she is the founder and president of DrDonnica.com, a leading women's health information website.

ELICIA MOORE lives in Monrovia, CA with her husband, Brian, and their three daughters, Kayla, Makaele, and Autumn. She enjoys volunteering at her kids' school, spending time with her family, and reading.

BARBARA NICHOLS and her husband, Kenny, live in Okeechobee, FL. She has a son, Matthew, who is in the army and a daughter, Carina, who is in middle school. She became a mom again at the age of forty-three, with daughter, Deborah.

Wife to Sean and mommy to Orion and Blaise, **ALISA NORRIS** is a stay-at-home mom living in Plano, TX. She works part-time for Talbots. Her hobbies include cleaning, changing diapers, doing dishes— Oh wait! That's just how she spends most of her time.

LAMIEL OESTERREICHER lives in Brooklyn, NY with her daughter, Maya Rose. During the day, they enjoy playing, running wild, and having the best time just doing nothing. After the toy piles and temper tantrums have subsided for the day, Lamiel enjoys spending free time chatting with friends, surfing the Net, and shopping on eBay.

DEBBIE PALMER lives in Hickory, NC with her two sons and husband, Lewis. She enjoys spending time with her family, working in the church nursery, cooking, and sewing.

LYNN PARKS lives in central North Carolina with husband, Andy, and son, Adam. When not volunteering at her son's school, Lynn can be found reading, quilting, or conversing with her online quilt group and friends.

STACI PARO'S home sweet home is in Massachusetts with the love of her life, Jon. Together, they are raising Handsome Prince Joshua and Beautiful Princess Julia. Let's not forget the Royal Jester Dog Zoe!

KRISTIN PENA, M.D., is a full-time mommy to daughter, Chloe, and part-time family practice physician in private practice. She lives with her daughter and husband, Paul, in beautiful Ventura, CA. When not working or entertaining Chloe, she enjoys reading, crafting, yoga, and traveling.

East Lansing, MI is home to **SARAH PLETCHER** and her son, Henry. She is entering her last year of medical school. In her spare time (ha!), she plays competitive tennis. She tells Henry every night that she must be the luckiest mama in the whole world to have him for a son.

TAMARA PRINCE is a counselor who lives in Oshawa, Ontario, Canada with her daughter and husband. Her hobbies include scrapbooking, hiking, and running.

TRACY PRITCHARD is a stay-at-home mom and full-time college student with her hands full. She lives in Kyle, TX with her husband, Matt, sons, Kane and Ryan, and daughter, Peyton. When she doesn't have her nose stuck in a textbook, Tracy can be found either mentoring elementary school students or playing her role of soccer mom to the fullest.

KRISZTINA RAB lives in Naperville, IL with her husband, Zoli, and son, Miki. They're expecting their second child. Krisztina works full-time as a tax attorney and enjoys swimming, reading, dancing, and singing.

CHAYA JAMIE REICH lives in Los Angeles, CA with her husband, Gideon, and daughter, Adele. She is a stay-at-home mom who enjoys gourmet cooking, reading classical literature, and watching *Bear in the Big Blue House*.

SHERRY RENNIE lives in Southern California with her two young sons and her husband of eight years. She is a committed stay-at-home mom who enjoys her menagerie of pets that include dogs, rats, reptiles, and fish. A good day consists of cleaning up less than two hundred messes and not having to say, "Don't pee on your brother!"

TESSICA REYNOLDS lives in Salt Lake City, UT with her husband, Jim, and their two boys, Jayden and Kody. They enjoy mountain biking in Moab, backcountry snowboarding, and shooting at defenseless paper targets!

KRISTINE RIVAS lives in Denver, CO with her husband, Sam, and baby, Isabella Noel. A full-time mommy as well as a financial services administrator outside the home, she enjoys children's songs, stories, and games.

MONIQUE RIVERA-ROGERS lives in Champaign, IL with her husband, Ryan, and son, Aidan. A work-at-home translator, she adores photographing her son's smile, sharing laughter with her husband, and cross-country road trips to visit family.

TANYA ROSARIO lives in the Bronx, NY with her husband, Francisco, and their son, Devin. She is a stay-at-home mom and a part-time student studying to become a court reporter.

JENNIFER ROSE lives in Ashland, MA with her husband, Eric, daughter, Becca, and son, Brian. Having recently completed a Master's degree, Jennifer works as a documentation specialist at a health care software company in Cambridge. In the warmer months, she enjoys softball and golf.

KARI RYDELL lives in Ladera Ranch, CA with her boys—husband, Paul, sons, Edward and James, and dog, Kirby. Aside from daily trips to the park, mall, grocery store, Gymboree, and playgroups, Kari is a full-time stay-at-home mom.

CAREN SADIKMAN, M.D., lives in Rochester, MN with her husband and her daughter, Sophia. She believes in showering children with hugs, love, and attention. She is a resident physician in physical medicine and rehabilitation and enjoys winding down at the end of the day by playing with Sophia, watching her taped soap opera, and eating ice cream.

DENINE SCALLEN is a stay-at-home mom who lives in Sammamish, WA with her husband and three sons. Her favorite activities are teaching her children to cook, painting, and jewelry making.

DIANNA SCHISSER lives in Frederick, MD with her husband, Trey, and son, Marq. A stay-at-home mom and member of the MOMS Club, her hobbies include photography, crafts, and sewing.

K. SCARLETT SHAW is a stay-at-home mom living in Euless, TX with her husband, Brad, and their son, Sam. She enjoys going to the park and flying kites, reading to her son—and herself—and crafting.

STACEY SKLAR lives in Oakland, CA with her husband, Eugene Hahm, and their daughters, Madeline and Lillian. She teaches high school English, does occasional freelance writing, and looks forward to eventually sleeping through the night undisturbed.

The proud wife of a U.S. Army officer, **THERESA SMEAD** is a stay-at-home/work-from-home mom of boy/girl twins residing in St. Louis, MO. She remembers cross-stitching and writing poetry as hobbies, but lately finds herself more amused with *Blue's Clues* and *Dora the Explorer.*

ANGEL SMITH runs a home-based business from the Brooksville, FL home she shares with her husband, Brian, son, Christian, stepson, Kristopher, and daughters, Emily and Faith. She is making plans to start a nonprofit organization focusing on outreach to teen mothers in her area and hopes to have a short story she's working on published next year.

BILLIE SMITH lives in Turpin, OK with her husband, Tim, and their daughter, Avery. A full-time executive assistant in local government, she enjoys photography, writing, and playing online checkers.

STEPHANIE R. SMITH resides in Northern Kentucky. She enjoys spending time outside with her husband, Rob, and daughters, Sydney, Ryan, and Sophie. She works as a supervisor at a large health care company in Cincinnati.

REBECCA SMONDROWSKI and her husband, Ken, live in Gaithersburg, MD with their children, Andrew and Sophia. On weekends, her schedule stays full with trips to Grandma's house, the beach, and the mountains.

ANGELA SNODGRASS is a creative homemaker and homeschooling mommy to three active little boys. She and her family live in the beautiful state of Idaho. In her free time (ha!) she enjoys scrapbooking, reading, and taking tea with friends.

KATE STEIMAN, part-time radio DJ, part-time area director for an au pair agency and full-time mom to Alicia, four, and Seth, two, lives with her traveling husband in Toms River, NJ. She originally hails from London, U.K.

RIVKA STEIN, M.D., is a pediatrician living in Brooklyn, NY. She has three children.

CHRISTINA K. STEVENS lives in Endicott, NY with her husband, Brad, and her sons, Alexander and Paris. She is a stay-at-home mom who cherishes her relationship with her children.

STACEY STEVENS lives in Alamo, CA with her husband, John Sweeney, and her two boys, Brendan and Kevin. In the five minutes each week that she is not chasing them around, Stacey is the vice president of the board of directors for the Valley Children's Museum.

AMELIA STINSON-WESLEY lives in Morganton, NC with her husband, Tom, and daughter, Kyra. An ordained United Methodist minister and executive director of a nonprofit organization, Amelia enjoys scrapbooking and traveling with her family.

ANN STOWE lives in Burlingame, CA with her husband, Nick, and their three children. She enjoys spending time with her family and friends. And in those rare free moments, she enjoys reading, cooking, going to the movies, and swimming.

LORI STUSSIE lives in Lawrence, KS with her husband, Larry, and three sons, Andrew, Cameron, and Noah. She is an English teacher at Lawrence Alternative High School and loves to read, scrapbook, and cheer for all Kansas University Jayhawk sports teams.

A work-from-home public relations manager, **JESSICA STYGLES** lives in Toledo, OH with her husband, Chris, and her two stunningly beautiful and brilliant daughters. She enjoys movies, punk concerts, and staying indoors as much as possible.

ANDREA SUISSA lives in Olney, MD with her husband, Dan, and her son, Alec, twin sons, Chase and Chad, and daughter, Samantha. When she is not working at her children's preschool, you can find her online or at the food store.

KAREN SULTAN lives in Rockville, MD with her husband, David, and sons, Jamey, Noah, and Coby. She is a part-time staff development teacher for Montgomery County Public Schools and enjoys reading, walking, and the theater.

KRISTI SWARTZ lives in Gaithersburg, MD with her husband, Dustin, and son, Brady. They are about to welcome baby number two to the family. A stay-at-home mom, her hobbies include cooking, baking, and shopping.

Palo Alto, CA is home to **SUSAN TACHNA,** her two sons and her husband, Steve. She spends her time chasing her two boys around, making sure that everyone is well fed, clothed, bathed, and tickled.

KRIS TAYLOR is currently living the life of her dreams as mommy to daughter, Kaedyn. She also moonlights as wife of Kaare and a full-time high school teacher in Dallas, TX. But it's the job of mommy she claims!

A stay-at-home mom, **KELI THAKUR** lives in Fort Wayne, IN with her husband, Deepankar, and daughter, Kamdyn. Currently expecting her second child, she enjoys relaxing with her family, spending time online, and shopping.

Norfolk, VA is home to **DEBORAH THERIAULT,** her husband, and daughter, Alyssa. She is trying to pursue a double degree in criminal justice and forensics. She enjoys horseback riding and getting outdoors.

Springboro, OH is home to **KRISTIN TOWNSEND** and her wonderful husband, Darrin, and two wonderful children, Dillon and Natalee. She works for a county children's service board in the hopes of making her job extinct one day.

SANDY TSAO, M.D., lives in Boston, MA with her amazing husband, Hensin, and her two incredible sons, Sebastian and Hunter. As Clinical Director of Cosmetic Dermatology and Laser Surgery at Massachusetts General Hospital, Harvard Medical School, her hobby is to make the world a prettier place in which to live.

TARA TUCKER lives in Mountain View, CA with her husband, David, and children, Katie and Michael. She left a professional career three years ago to become a full-time mom, a job she loves more than she ever imagined she could.

BROOKE ULINSKI is a work-at-home mom to three kids, Mikey, DJ, and Ashlyn. She lives in Levittown, PA. She enjoys spending time with her family, reading, and playing with her kids in the backyard.

A stay-at-home mom, **LORI VANCE** and her husband live in Henderson, NV with their boy/girl twins.

CARA VINCENS is a Canadian mom living in Thionville, France with her husband, Matthieu, and her two boys, Jacques and Anthony. She loves photography and takes tons of pictures of her favorite subjects: her boys!

KAREN EISENHART WANG, M.D., lives in Wayne, PA with her husband, Bryan, and son, Simon. A part-time pediatrician, she enjoys reading, cooking, crafts, and spending time with friends.

BEVERLY WAXLER, M.D., lives and works in the Chicagoland area of Illinois with her husband and son, now twenty years old. She started a residency in anesthesiology when her son was seventeen months old. She is now active in caring for patients, teaching residents, and doing research.

COLLEEN GRACE WEAVER lives in San Lorenzo, CA with her husband, Chris, and daughters, Christian Jeanette and Cassandra Ray. She is an advocate of attachment parenting and breastfeeding. Colleen works full-time in marketing and holds a certificate in opticianry.

JENNIFER WEINTRAUB lives in Dallas, TX with her husband, Chuck, and their daughter, Samantha. Now a stay-at-home mom, Jennifer tries to find time to be a good mom, make other mommy friends, work on her photography, and ride her horse, the last remnant of her previous life.

VERONICA WILSON is a twenty-five-year-old pediatric nursing student who lives in Chattanooga, TN with her two sons. Loving her children and seeing their happiness is enough to make her feel that everything she has done works just perfectly.

JULIA WONDERLING lives outside of Philadelphia, PA with her two daughters and wonderful husband, Eric. She is in her fourth year of medical school, with the goal of becoming an emergency medicine physician. She enjoys spending time with her family and working on projects around the house.

JUDITH WU lives in Orange, CA with her husband, Alex, and son, Brandon. They have a daughter on the way. A stay-at-home mom, she enjoys scrapbooking, cooking, chilling out at home, hanging out with friends, and, of course, sleeping.

JENNIFER YOUNG lives in Bethesda, MD with her husband, John, and two children. Her dream date includes a meal cooked AND SERVED by someone else, without having to stop every two minutes to say, "Will you please keep your bottom in the chair," and "Don't forget to eat your vegetables."

STEPHANIE ZARA lives in Boonton Township, NJ with her husband, George, and their daughter, Mary Alice. An artist, painter, and photographer, she and her husband believe in attachment parenting, extended breastfeeding, delaying solids, and that strong family bonds and a loving home are essential to a happy, healthy, loving family.

TIFFANY ZIMMER lives in Baltimore, MD with her husband, Mike, and her two children, Catie and Flynn. She started her own accounting business after the birth of her first child. She works out of her home, so she can spend as much time as she can with her kids. In her spare time, she enjoys . . . wait a minute! What is spare time?

INDEX